Fashion Zeitgeist

July 2008

Fashion Zeitgeist

Trends and Cycles in the Fashion System

Barbara Vinken

Translated by Mark Hewson

Oxford • New York

English edition
First published in 2005 by
Berg
Editorial offices:
First Floor, Angel Court, 81 St Clements Street, Oxford OX4 1AW, UK
175 Fifth Avenue, New York, NY 10010, USA

Berg is the imprint of Oxford International Publishers Ltd.

Library of Congress Cataloging-in-Publication Data

Vinken, Barbara, 1960–
    Fashion zeitgeist : trends and cycles in the fashion system / Barbara Vinken ; translated by
Mark Hewson. — English ed.
        p. cm.
    Includes bibliographical references and index.
    ISBN 1-84520-043-8 (cloth) — ISBN 1-84520-044-6 (pbk.)
    1. Fashion design—History. 2. Fashion—History. 3. Fashion designers—History. I. Title.

    TT507.V58 2005
    391'.009—dc22

                                                                            2004020615

British Library Cataloguing-in-Publication Data

A catalogue record for this book is available from the British Library.

ISBN 1 84520 043 8 (hardback)
        1 84520 044 6 (paperback)

Typeset by JS Typesetting Ltd, Wellingborough, Northants
Printed in the United Kingdom by Biddles Ltd, King's Lynn.

www.bergpublishers.com

Contents

List of Figures

Part I

Postfashion

1

What Fashion Strictly Divided

Fashion has rarely enjoyed a very good reputation. Despite its undeniable success as a social and commercial phenomenon, it remains the very exemplum of superficiality, frivolity and vanity. The discourse on fashion assumes the philosophical form of a critique of mere appearances, the cultural-theoretical form of a critique of the market-economy, or the traditional form of a critique of sexual morality; but there seems to be no possibility of a serious concern with the subject that would proceed otherwise than in the mode of critique.

Glittering and blinding, fashion draws attention away from the substance of things. It is the very personification of the individual alienated in the rush of consumption, of the self lost in the brilliant world of commodities. Irrational, capricious, fickle, unpredictable, fashion makes its entrance every season anew, with all the power of seduction of a moody sovereign, certain of conquering. The incarnation of all vanity in the world, it carries with it the *odor di femmina*, of which Don Giovanni sings. The philosophers and the sociologists take it up only in order to denounce it or, at best, contemplate it with a wry and distanced amusement.

The discourse on fashion is constructed by the correlation of three major conceptual articulations: the division of being and mere appearance; the division of the sexes; and – inseparably linked to the latter – the division of the classes. In modern times, there has been a marked tendency for the first of these conceptualities – whether it appears in its philosophical form or in its ethical application – to be incorporated into the sociological variations of the divisions of gender and class. This phenomenon of compression has been compounded by the fact that the paradigm of the division of the sexes has allowed itself to be grafted onto the discourse on class, dominant until the eighteenth century, with the same ease that, in traditional thought, the moral condemnation of vanity let itself be combined with the philosophical suspicion of mere appearance.

In what follows, I propose to read the dominant sociological discourse on fashion as symptomatically expressing the containment and the repression of the phenomenon which it seeks to explain. Fashion is, no doubt, sociology's darling. The most influential analyses of fashion have been done from a sociological perspective. This is a discourse that even in its most advanced stances, like, let's say, that of Bourdieu, remains true to the logic of representation: fashion represents class and gender – a given that has only to be expressed. Against this model of representation, as featured in the sociological analysis, I would like to analyze fashion as a poetological activity that, like any poetological discourse, thematizes itself and has performative power. Fashion not only confirms and economically functionalizes the division of gender and class; it constructs and subverts them by stripping them bare – if this clothing metaphor is allowed here – and reveals them as an effect of construction.

Recently, the sociological discourse analyzed here has been qualified as unfashionable.[1] It will become apparent that fashion, the object of the containment and repression, can be said to fulfill the tasks allocated to it by sociological theory, but only in a highly paradoxical way. It does indeed set up gender and class divisions; it does not, however, certify these as natural, but rather exposes them as artificial. It is only in the comforting analyses of the sociologists of fashion that fashion confirms the order of things, and leaves the politics of the day undisturbed.

In fact – and this will be my claim – fashion is the site at which this politics is non-conceptually but ostentatiously exposed at its weak point – that is, at the point at which it is a sexual politics.

In Thorstein Veblen's now classical theory of the leisure class, the woman represents the wealth of her husband; she is characterized as *mobilia*, as the mobile property of her husband.[2] She is the index of his economic situation, the prestige-object of a household, who is ceaselessly occupied in the task of creating fine distinctions.[3] Because the woman, 'perhaps in a highly idealized sense, … is still the man's chattel,' is still economically dependent on him, and is, in a sense, his first servant, her clothes, precisely adjusted to the rapid change of fashions, represent his power of purchase. But more than this, they also underline her idleness. At the expense of her comfort, her clothes render her physically incapable of work.[4] Her function consists in exhibiting his fortune; her appearance exhibits his being. She represents his wealth in the opulence of her clothes, in the rapid transitions of fashion, but also with her body, which exhibits, by its manner of dress, its unsuitability for work, and announces, by its physical desireability, that it is well maintained.

Fashion has never more rigorously divided the sexes than in the nineteenth century. 'His' eternally inconspicuous dark suit provides the ideal matt background before which 'she' can spring into life, with the brilliance of silk, the sparkle of jewels, the shimmer of naked skin, and the ivory of the *décolleté* (Figure 1). The affluence of the man, understated in charcol grey cloth, is all the more impressive thanks to the jewel at his side, an object of display floating in silk and furs, hung with jewelry and dazzling in bright colors.

For Veblen, fashion works to separate the classes in that it intro-duces a strict division between the sexes in the leisure class. It is not only the vehicle of this separation, however, but at the same time, the vehicle for possible transgressions.

There are of course also free men, and not a few of them who, in their blind zeal for faultlessly reputable attire, transgress the theoretical line between man's and woman's dress, to the extent of arraying themselves in apparel that is obviously designed to vex the mortal frame; but everyone recognizes without hesitation that such apparel for men is a departure from the normal. We are in the habit of saying

Figure 1
Jean Béraud, *Une soirée,*
1878, © Photo RMN – H.
Lewandowski.

that such dress is 'effeminate'; and one sometimes hears the remark that such or such an exquisitely attired gentleman is as well dressed as a footman.[5]

One finds a very similar judgment in Simone de Beauvoir. The fact that it is existentially rather than sociologically formulated makes no great difference in this context, and speaks at the most for the high degree of interiorization of which the phenomenon is susceptible. What for Veblen was imposed on the woman by her objective economic status – although 'not a few men' voluntarily submitted themselves to the same imposition – is for de Beauvoir, seventy years later, something that women undertake out of their own free will and for their own pleasure. Through fashion, the woman alienates herself from herself: 'When she has accepted her vocation as a sexual object, then she gladly adorns herself,' she 'costumes herself to the pleasure of all men, and to the pride of her owner.' Where the man claims transcendence through his clothing, and does not allow his body to hold the gaze, she chooses the being of the empty appearance, pure, blinding exteriority.[6] But here too some men overstep the clear dividing lines between the sexes. A certain proportion of the exceptions are accounted for by de Beauvoir with the term pederast. With respect to the enigma of the other part, of the fashion-conscious dandy, Beauvoir concedes that the subject 'would require an independent inquiry.' Indeed.

From Veblen and Simmel to König and Bourdieu, there has been a consistent – even a desperate – attempt to describe fashion as functioning to divide the classes and the sexes, and therefore to maintain the social order. But when it comes to concretely demonstrating this, the critical discourse always gets tangled up in the kind of contradictions that mark the examples taken from Veblen and de Beauvoir. One such stumbling block, which regularly reappears at critical moments in historical treatments of fashion, is the *demi-monde*, the world of the dandy and the coquette, which flourished at the birthplace of fashion in modernity, in the Second Empire of Napoleon III. Marx assigns a central role in his salvational scheme to this phenomenon. Having attained power with (and in) Napoleon III, the *demi-monde*, which stands outside the order of class and gender, represents for Marx the necessary terminal phase of bourgeois capitalism. As a preliminary to the emergence of the new, in the form of the proletarian revolution, capitalism here brings itself to an end – through a 'farce,' as Marx says, which follows upon the 'tragedy' of the Revolution.[7] 'Play it again Sam' could be the motto for the 18th Brumaire, in which the history of the West gives one last performance, and, through a travesty of all its previous performances, definitively attains its end. The *demi-monde*, in which the separation of classes and of sexes is perverted, this time – following Marx – irreparably, is the agent of this travesty. As the necessary preliminary stage to the proletarian revolution, which is to bring about the radical break with the structure of all previous history, Marx welcomes the phenomenon, even if he finds it absurd, and describes it, in tones reminiscent of Rousseau, as a society in which men sell themselves to other men like courtesans, and in which heterosexuality and masculinity both go by the board.[8] In Marx's description of the *demi-monde*, one sees elements of the traditional moral condemnation of fashion coalescing with the new, post-revolutionary (1792) sexual politics. The revolutionary potential of the asociality of the *demi-monde* is dependent on the regime which it travesties.

The sociology of fashion, caught in the paradox of its *demi-mondaine* substrata, has taken no notice of the prehistory of this travesty. Instead, sociological discourse has produced ever new variations on the deep-rooted moral condemnation of fashion, a reaction repeated in the existentialist, and later in a certain part of the feminist discourse on fashion. Documents of the categorical rejection of fashion, viewed as an allegory of the vanity of Dame World, span the whole history of the topic, from the Old Testament up until late modernity. The same standpoint is expressed by a social revolutionary like Savonarola in the Florence of the fifteenth century on the one hand, and in the edifying remarks of Mme de Maintenon, the later favorite of Louis XIV, on the other. Against the false beauty of appearances stands the truth of the other world. The brilliant ornament, the splendid crimson, the long rustling train of a dress, the lace-fitted seductive low-cut neckline, the luxurious golden hair that flows from the shimmering head-wear, all of this only snares one in the false joys of the profane world, for which we deprive ourselves of the true and permanent joys of the other world.[9] The censures are not just directed at the so-called fairer sex, but also at the addiction to finery of the stronger sex, which in the pre-revolutionary moment adorned itself more finely than was later to be the custom. The beauty of a male leg, the play of the calf and of the thigh, advantageously set off in flesh-colored, skintight boots or finely embroidered silk stockings; the gleaming white of the complexion underlined by the luxurious lace; the genitals impressively emphasized by expensively embroidered velvet and silk inlays: the codpiece that leaves nothing to be desired in terms of its proportions, ornamentation and magnifying realism. From the slits of trousers of the Spanish grandees as later from those of the German estate-servants, a lining made from a hundred cubits of silk flowed so luxuriously that 'when the trouser-heroes passed, there was a sound like the river Elbe running over a bridge or over a weir.'[10]

Although the moral objection to fashion was, as such, perhaps, never particularly compelling, it was able to strengthen itself by drawing on a political objection. In the ideological elaborations of the republican democracy in the eighteenth century, fashion becomes a point of intersection between the division of classes and the division of sexes – a point of crisis and a symptom for a new order of things. Fashion, vanity and luxury – but also the emergence of women with political influence into the public sphere – become the signature of the obsolete political form of the monarchy. The traditional symptoms of moral decay become symptoms of political decline. The corrupt, softened – i.e. feminized – monarchy is confronted with a manly republic, sworn to virtue. The Republic envisages itself as an order of simplicity and rigor. Along with equality and fraternity, it proclaims the disappearance of the feminine out of the public sphere. In the woman, then, fashion, vanity and luxury find not only their natural bearer, but also their political representative. Against the kind of men who had to advance the cause of their career and ambition on an individual basis, *via* women, i.e. *via* seduction, there emerges now the 'individual universal' (Kant) of the men who live entirely by the general will and who subordinate their individual interests to the interest of the Republic.

A monarchy needs subjects, subjected to the king, but a republic needs free men – thus Rousseau, the prime ideologue of the new political discourse. In his reflections on women, luxury and fashion, and on their corrupting influence on the cause of the free, equal and brotherly Republic, he has an illustrious predecessor in Montesquieu, whose diagnosis leaves nothing to be desired in terms of clarity.

> The society of the fair sex spoils the manners and forms the taste; the desire of giving greater pleasure than others establishes the embellishments of dress; and the desire of pleasing others more than ourselves gives rise to fashions. Thus fashion is a subject of importance; by encouraging a trifling turn of mind, it continually increases the branches of its commerce.[11]

This does not make things any better, it merely unmasks a characteristic trait of monarchy.

> In monarchies women are subject to very little restraint, because as the distinction of ranks calls them to court, there they assume a spirit of liberty, which is almost the only one tolerated in that place. Each courtier avails himself of their charms and passions, in order to advance his fortune: and as their weakness admits not of pride, but of vanity, luxury constantly attends them.[12]

With women idleness, luxury, gallantry and *libertinage* reign. Their domain is a domain of vice. Men are forced to submit to an empty arbitrary tyranny, in order to avoid being judged ridiculous.

In such a society, exclusively determined by appearance, catastrophe cannot be far away, for here the difference between the sexes threatens to be erased. The desire of the women to please and that of the men to please them in return lead to both sexes losing their essential distinctive properties. It may be ridiculous when women become men, but it is horrifying to see men turn into women. Rousseau sees this perversion in the Babel that cities have become, where the public influence of women has turned men into slaves in a seraglio owned by women. 'Unable to make themselves into men, the women make us into women,'[13] declares Rousseau. A determinate political discourse will henceforth no longer be separable from a discourse on gender and sexuality. A particular social class of men – the nobles – and a particular form of sovereignty – the monarchy – are characterized by a lack of masculinity: Marx edifies himself with this observation. In the monarchy, men have to disguise themselves as women. This sickness spreads like a plague, and even threatens the pure, free republican, and not least, Reformed Geneva: 'On my last trip to Geneva I already saw several of these young ladies in jerkins [Rousseau is describing young men], with white teeth, plump hands, piping voices, and pretty green parasols in their hand, rather maladroitly counterfeiting men.'[14]

The *justaucorps*, the tight-fitting jacket associated with the nobility, confirms the suspicion of femininity in the age of the loose-fitting woolen cloth coat of the bourgeois, introduced from England. Nobility and femininity have in common an emphasis on the body, which is not, however, fitting for the citizen. The success of Rousseau's rhetoric is reflected in a decree that makes unmistakably clear who wears the trousers in the post-revolutionary republic. In the 8th Brumaire of the year II (29 October 1793), women are prohibited from wearing long pants. The revolution of 1789 is also, and not least, a revolution in fashion, and it creates a long-lasting revolutionary potential for fashion, which will eventually destroy the order of the sexes that the revolution has instituted.

Henceforth, the citizen-man – the only real man – stands in a negative relation to the world of frivolous appearance. He *is*. Therefore he does not need to appear nor to represent. The ability to identify oneself with the masculine leads to the standardization of male clothing. In contrast to the masculine body of the court, the bourgeois masculine body is not sexually marked. Every masculine display of sexual beauty is proscribed. All the ornaments of masculinity come to an end with the new drainpipe trousers. Balzac's *Physiology of Fashion* aptly describes this tendency.[15] From the Revolution a segregationist society emerges, in which the sharpest line of demarcation is no longer horizontal – noble or non-noble – but vertical – man or woman. Fashion becomes a synonym for femininity.[16]

The nineteenth century was characterized as the century of 'masculine renunciation.'[17] To the extent to which he renounces fashion and adopts the simplistic rhetoric of anti-rhetoric, the man gains identity, authenticity, unquestioned masculinity, seriousness. To be sure, it is a matter even here of a characteristic non-simultaneity of the simultaneous. And it is again the court that – after revolution – insists on bringing noble, representative masculinity as a historical surplus and relic from a bygone age into civilian uniforms whose splendor nowadays seems more like a curiosity. Upon the occasion of an exhibition of the wardrobe of the Viennese court from the time of Sisi and Franz Josef, *Figaro Magazine* emphasized the magnificence of the parade uniforms. Richly embroidred, studded with pearls, turquoise and silver, and lined with mink and panther, they were equal in their splendor to the women's wardrobes. These uniforms are relics from the imperial and, in the strictest sense, the pre-modern and pre-fashionable, non-bourgeois period, which, in their aggressive withdrawal from modern life, represent a peculiar outlet of suppressed tendencies. In a constant state of exception in bourgeois times, the uniformed man marks a masculine sexuality that is not particularly emphasized by the bourgeois unit. Where the aristocratic feminine or the heroic solitary dandy are wrapped up in frivolity, and ostentatiously resist all functionalization, the masculinity that clothes itself in uniform aligns itself with a strictly hierarchized and functionalizable collectivity. Although in themselves pre-modern phenomena, uniforms, owing to their massive presence in bourgeois society, have a unique status in that they represent the only place where masculinity is literally 'on parade.' At least until the perfection, after the two world wars, of the camouflage-uniform according to the ideal of the guerilla, the uniform maintains something of the display of splendor characteristic of the nobility.

It is the uniform's uniform suitability for the masses that has made possible its reappearance in the fashion of the modern. The body that was first standardized and measured was that of the soldier in the Prussian army. The military's norming and standardization of the human body according to sizes – still four at that time, the so-called stomach sizes of the officers not included – is the *sine qua non* of the *prêt-à-porter*.[18] Modern fashion is, to a certain extent, tailored after the uniform.

Beyond the technical measure that is provided by the uniformity of uniforms, uniforms offer a wealth of references as diverse as they are puzzling – from the blue admiral's jacket with gold buttons and gold stripes on the arm, combined with white pants for both men and women, all the way to the martial uniform-rags in the fashion of Gaultier. Within the masculine-homosexual spectrum, the quasi-uniformed, ultra-macho men – culminating in *Tom's men* – form the counterpart to queens and fairies; they constantly stress that one can be queer without being feminine; rather one can be a complete man, a real man, more masculine than other men. This ostentation of the more masculine, this excess of staging and presentation, this 'having too much' and 'being more' does not fail to awaken the suspicion that one is somehow lacking in substantial maleness.

The citizen-man, who renounces all sexuality marked by clothes, is able to escape this threat. Clothing never divided the sexes more rigidly than in the nineteenth century. Not only did men and women clothe themselves very differently; it was above all the relationship of clothing to gender that was different – with the strange exceptions of the dandy and the uniform. 'Masculine' meant unmarked gender; 'feminine' meant marked sexuality.

This purely historical alignment of femininity and marked sexuality *qua* fashion versus masculinity and unmarked sexuality *qua* indifference to fashion has virtually attained the status of an anthropological given. This is amply demonstrated by Richard Alewyn's description of aristocratic men's fashion of the seventeenth and eighteenth centuries. Colorful, resplendent, richly ornamented with ribbons, bows, lace and feathers, studded with pearls, precious stones and valuable buttons, and embroidered with gold, the clothing of the masculine nobility at the court of Louis XIV appears 'effeminate' to him: the man, usurping the female sphere, decorated himself, as the woman did, in order to be an ornament. His status at court, like hers, was determined by appearance. Entirely in the tradition of republican discourse, Alewyn attributes this confusion of spheres to the nobility's loss of power. Since the nobility was no longer what it once had been, nothing else remained for it but to play as if, to make believe.[19] The man of the eighteenth century, the man of court, who did not yet appear as earnestly unrefined as his bourgeois successor, but was rather the equal of the ladies of the court in gracefulness and elegance, was seen in age of the bourgeoisie as effeminate and grovelling.[20] Such a standpoint completely overlooks the fact that the feudal nobility of the Renaissance, which clothed itself no less magnificently than its courtly successors, is immune to any argument based on deprivation of power. One thinks of the tight velvet trousers, the full feathered hats, the expensively embroidered jerkins of velvet and silk and the colorful and diverse patterns of the codpieces. Historians such as Alewyn decode the epoch before the historical shift according to the standards of our contemporary codes of gender and representation. Lacan's dictum that the parade of the masculine, virile display itself appears as feminine is as correct for the bourgeois epoch as it is false for the feudal epoch.[21]

Hence it is that in reference to gender relations, we find ourselves in the bourgeois period, if not in a completely new situation, then at least in a radicalized one. The constitutive social divide no longer opposes the noble and the non-noble, but rather the feminine and the masculine. The opposition feminine/masculine is doubled, however, by a second opposition, that of noble and bourgeois. Here noble has become a metaphor for the appearance of power. The bourgeoisie uses its women to exhibit the castration of the nobility. The all-determining opposition that constitutes sexual difference is now that of authentic and inauthentic. Men 'are' – they are someone, they are authentic, real; women on the other hand lack essence and are sheer appearance, artificial, inauthentic. Fashion appears as something that is excluded from the apparently non-rhetorical authenticity of the bourgeois masculine collective. Drawing together femininity and nobility on the basis of their shared frivolity of appearance, it thus excludes them from the real world in which men dwell, securely enclosed within the institutions of masculinity.

As men increasingly assume the clothing of the professions, women begin to dress as 'women.' Men produce, women consume; men work, women cultivate idleness and the social amusements. The more securely men divide up the power among themselves, the more liberally the noble attributes of dominance are transferred to the woman. She becomes the absolute sovereign of hearts. With the separation of the sexes and the exclusion of women from the political, productive and public sphere, consumption, luxury and vanity are defused of their dangerous power. Fused into a collective, men are no longer susceptible to the virus women carry, no longer threatened in their masculinity. Luxury and vanity are simply the proof of the childishness and immaturity of women – not vices corrupting the whole of society, merely weaknesses, which at least give women something with which to occupy themselves, and prevent them from concerning themselves with more serious matters. Within liberal capitalism, on the other hand, fashion is taken seriously, as the substantial economic factor which it doubtless is: in the interplay of private vices, a public virtue is generated, just as Mandeville, in his *Fable of the Bees*, had foreseen.[22]

As Georg Simmel saw clearly in his famed essay of 1911, the *demi-monde*, as 'pioneer of fashion,' is the other side of the coin. Or so it has seemed at least to the sociologists who, after Simmel, have written the sociologies of fashion. Already with Simmel, the contradictions with which sociology will be preoccupied at least until its semiotic turning with Barthes are fully developed. The *demi-monde*, as the milieu from which fashion receives its decisive impulse, is its stumbling block. For Simmel, it is not least the particularly modern tempo of fashion, the restless movement of constant change, which gives this impulse expression. The whirlwind movement of fashion suggests an 'open or latent hatred of everything that is already legalized, fixed in a stable form'; this hatred, Simmel continues, comes from a peculiarly deracinated life form, from the 'paria-existence' of the *demi-monde*, and finds in fashion the relatively harmless 'aesthetic form of the destructive instinct.'[23] The problem then is how fashion, despite this origin, can nonetheless be conceived as representing and supporting its opponent, namely the established order.

Since Simmel links fashion to the post-monarchical epoch, the relation of fashion and democratic social structures has to move to the center point of sociological investigations of the phenomenon. Fashion serves the cause of distinction and at the same time that of equality, making it possible for individuals to stand out, and yet at the same time to reference their social belonging. Insofar as fashion is based on imitation, it seems to be a deeply affirmative form of social conduct, one that serves communication and that has to remain compatible with it, even in the case of those who would claim indifference to fashion in the strong sense. For the sociology of fashion, fashion has not only to represent the structure of democracy, but also the natural order of society. It is to bring sameness and differentiations ideally to expression and *de facto* to reproduce the divisions into classes and sexes. In a form of contradictory subordination to the ideal, fashions remain always, for sociology, class-fashions. Their real goal would be to set off the higher classes from the lower classes; they are abandoned at the moment in which the latter begin to appropriate them.[24]

Precisely through its rapid changes, fashion guarantees stability, since it reconciles within itself the merely apparent contradictions of democracy. In the final analysis, fashion confirms democracy as the legitimate ongoing order. Such is the deceptive result of sociological theory, which denies that which makes the harmony falter; this analysis falls prey to the aporia that it has to locate the forces that drive fashion outside of fashion. The dandy is, for René König, unquestionably the driving force behind the emergence of new fashions. But for him the 'fashion snob' or dandy is not the epitome of fashion, but only a marginal case of fashion-behavior, 'one who exaggerates the general social function of fashion to the point where it finally becomes self-contradictory.'[25] The admission of self-contradiction cooperates with an unfortunate failure on the part of the borderline figure of the dandy, in order to preserve the functioning of the assumed communicative act. The fashion-snob's concern, for König, can only be that of dissolving into the mainstream of society, but he sends out signals of a distinction which cannot be received by the rest of society. He is too far in advance. He is the unfortunate symptom of a movement, whose law is the social justification of fashion, fashionable distinctions as society-forming function.

The jurist Rudoph von Ihering, immortalized in Walter Benjamin's *Passagenwerk*, devoted an extensive description to the priority of the 'social motive.' It is not least the discovery of this motive which calls sociology as science into action, concerning the 'purpose in law':

Nevertheless, fashion, as we understand it today, has no individual motives but only a social motive... This motive is the effort to distinguish the higher classes of society from

the lower, or more especially from the middle classes...
Fashion is the barrier – continually raised anew because
continually torn down – by which the fashionable world
seeks to segregate itself from the middle region of society;
it is the mad pursuit of that class vanity through which a
single phenomenon endlessly repeats itself: the endeavour
of one group to establish a lead, however minimal, over its
pursuers, and the endeavour of the other group to make up
the distance by immediately adopting the newest fashions
of the leaders... Fashion moves from top to bottom, not
vice versa... Any attempt by the middle classes to introduce
a new fashion would ... never succeed, though nothing
would suit the upper classes better than to see the former
with their own set of fashions.[26]

'Fashion passes from the top down.' It would seem only appropriate to the standing of the ruling class. That it is *de facto*
otherwise is shown in a punctually registered afterthought,
although without this flagrant contradiction causing too much
grief to the author: 'Which does not deter them from looking for
new designs in the sewer of the Parisian demi-monde and bringing
out fashions that clearly bear the mark of their unseemly origins,
as F. Th. Vischer... has pointed out in his ... widely censured,
but to my mind, ... highly meritorious essay on fashion.'[27]

Benjamin cites Ihering after the *Illustrierte Sittengeschichte*
of Eduard Fuchs, who for his part balances the offense, which
Vischer in every respect took, against Ihering's sociological
discovery: the 'erotic problem of clothing.' Fashion seems no
longer able to fulfill its function of class division, as far as the
female sex is concerned. On the contrary, it becomes precisely
the site in which the division of rank is overcome. The erotic
problem of clothing signaled by Vischer is that, in regard to
clothing, one can no longer well distinguish between a virtuous
woman and a courtesan. Benjamin cites to this effect extensively
from Charles Blanc, from 1872, and also from Egon Friedell,
from 1931, whose more succinct diagnosis reads: 'The paragon
of fashion is the *grande dame* who plays the cocotte.'[28]

This is perhaps not such a problem for the history of culture and
moeurs, built up, as it is, out of curiosities, but for sociological
inquiry it is more difficult. Fashion is, from this standpoint, only
a harmless, aesthetic vehicle for the aggressions of those who are

strangely without social being; it can even be a substitute for that which 'is denied to the personality to attain on a purely individual basis.'[29] Simmel envisages this substitute above all for women: 'from the weakness of the social position to which women were for far the large part of history condemned, it necessarily follows that they have a close relationship to custom.' Fashion assigns them their place, which only the 'cynicism' lacking all decency, denounced by Vischer, would wish to eliminate. On the other hand, the flight into 'concealing leveling,' or 'blind obedience' to fashion on the part of 'fine and peculiar natures' (of the male sex, one has to understand here) can also serve as mask; then it protects the inalienable personal element, the core of a true being, which uses this outer covering to withdraw itself from the profane gaze of the public space. Under the mantle of custom, fashion protects outstanding individuals (i.e. male individuals) by disguising them as average, while it compensatorily lends individual distinctions to those (female) individuals whose lack of identity would otherwise cause them to be swallowed up in the masses.

The discourse of sociology is a discourse of representation, which protects the essential, the true and the natural. It is a defense against forms of appearance, such as literature, art and also fashion. Sociology represses, at the point at which repression is most needed, and it is no wonder that fashion became its favorite adoptive child. But where does this leave that disturbing class from which fashion draws its inspiration? Marx has a clearer estimate of the destructive potential of the *demi-monde* than the sociology that succeeds him, oriented, as it is, toward the preservation of the existing conditions. What the *demi-monde* primarily destroys – and this is no less tolerable for Marx than it is for sociology – is the opposition of being and appearance, of *Sein* and *Schein*. The field in which the *demi-monde* did and still does this is fashion. Along the lines of Marx, one could say that fashion mobilizes the division of the sexes in such a way as to drive the separation of classes to its end. This it does for its own purposes, however. As much as it may be condemned for its indifference to ethical and political purposes, fashion remains a disruption of the political and, as such, cannot be other than political.

Fashion divides, according to the received consensus. It divides classes from one another; but it also divides the individual – and especially the female individual – from herself. Fashion is a seductive and distracting force, driving the self to abandon itself to the lures of the world. But it is in relation to the sexes that the power of division worked by fashion is at its most effective and its most complex. Fashion divides, but it also, uncannily, erases the division of the sexes, and then ostentatiously displays the traces of the division that once was there. Constantly marking, erasing and transgressing borders, fashion withdraws itself from orderly social categories, makes for a disturbance, creates excitement and anxiety. Here for once, exceptions do not confirm the rule. Rather, they render impossible forms of analysis that proceed from the 'normal case.' The dandy is just such a non-normal case, one who undermines the social separation of the sexes. The *haute couture* takes its measure from him. It appears at the moment at which the division of the sexes is at its most extreme. Far from cementing this division, the *haute couture* deconstructs it. It is nothing other than the play with the boundaries between the sexes, with the normativized signs that regulate the sexual difference. As a commentary on the limits fixed through clothing and on clothing, the *haute couture* is a discourse in clothing about clothing. It is deeply linked, even identical, to the transgression of gender identity. It was not until the 1960s that *haute couture* lost this power; by the 1980s it had made the transition to *prêt-à-porter*.

The view that fashion does no more than confirm and economically functionalize the division of genders and gender roles that lies at the origin of the post-revolutionary modern order is entirely superficial. In fact, the effect of fashion has been ultimately to deconstruct the opposition between a brotherly rivalry of producing, working, political men and a vain, extravagant, idle femininity. Certainly, at a primary level, fashion is intended to exhibit an opposition of this form. In their women, the bourgeoisie exhibit the castration of the nobility. But this had uncontrollable counter-effects: the sparks of ruin sprung over from the nobility to the male bourgeois world, which had believed itself safely at a distance. Art, the dandy, fashion, have been, since the second half of the nineteenth century, subversive forces, undermining the modern order: of these, fashion alone has survived. It draws its vitality, not from the critique of the prevailing social and political conditions (this critique having been extinguished in art as in literary life), but from its relation to the division of the sexes, which fashion considers to be a matter of visible signs that can be manipulated and reversed.[30]

La mode de cent ans: in the second half of the nineteenth century, three phenomena originate almost simultaneously – a new aesthetic doctrine: *l'art pour l'art*; a new type of man: the dandy; and a new form of creation: fashion design becomes an autonomous art form. The main representatives of *l'art pour l'art* are at the same time dandies and theoreticians of fashion. The poets of this period, from Gautier to Mallarmé, from Baudelaire to Barbey d'Aurevilly, devote themselves intensively to fashion. Under a pseudonym, Mallarmé produces eight issues of a fashion magazine by himself: *La dernière mode – Gazette du monde et de la famille* appears from 6 September to 20 December 1874. In Gautier and D'Aurevilly, the dandy is no effeminate fool: in Gautier's *Fortunio* (1837) he appears as an aesthetic rebel and an intellectual hero. His fashion-consciousness is an index of a new aristocratic taste, one that antagonizes the utilitarian values of bourgeois society by its devotion to the fine detail. In Baudelaire's *Peintre de la Vie Moderne* fashion becomes expressly what it had been latently in Gautier: the paradigm of a modern poetics.

The first artist of this new art was Charles Frederick Worth (1825–95). 'The fashions that intrigued Gautier in 1858, fascinated Baudelaire in 1860, and preoccupied Mallarmé in 1874 were thus all by-products of the House of Worth. More than any individual poet or painter, Charles Worth succeeded in creating an aura around fashion and promoting it as a new art for modern times.'[31] Specialists of fashion from Anne Hollander to Diana de Marley concur with this judgment from a recent literary history. It was Worth who transformed fashion from a craft to an art. In 1840 he came from London to Paris; in 1855 his clothes won first prize in the World Exhibition; in 1858 he opened his own fashion house in the rue de la Paix; and in 1863 he became official tailor to the imperial court, whose fall he very successfully survived. In the Third Republic, his domination was more uncontested than ever. The legendary rise of the House of Worth was not moreover – as is now all too willingly accepted in a widely circulating commonplace – owing or even primarily due to the alteration in the conditions of production, which took place in the Second Empire, but rather to an artistic sense which knew how to make itself a career under these conditions.

Until that time the woman of society would choose a material, and send it to the fashion designer with an idea for its cut. For Worth, however, the cut of the dress, the material and the pattern of the cloth belonged inseparably together. The result was that fashion production was concentrated in one house. At the same time, mass production became possible. Until this time, every article of clothing had been unique; now, as a model, it could be exactly reproduced at will. The wearer no longer exhibited her own taste, but that of her fashion designer; she practically became his mannequin. She clothed herself no longer in her own name but in his. While in the Ancien Régime, the queen, Marie Antoinette, displayed the art of the unknown fashion designer Rose Bertin, and thereby demonstrated her own good taste, the Emperess Eugénie proved her taste in that she chose the taste of Worth and wore it in his name. In the firmament of fashion, it is no longer the names of a small number of women which shine, but the names of the fashion designers.

Worth's revolution was that he sold under his own name. Indeed it was, in a sense, his name that he sold. This name was not a natural given: it had to be produced. Until this point, the only possibility of acquiring a name, for those not born with one, had been as an artist: to win a name by the uniqueness of the work, the signature of the style. Worth stylized himself as a genius, an eccentric, inspired artist; he neglected none of the classical circumstances of the artist's life: he relished crises of creativity, darker moods, fits of melancholy, and would be overtaken by sudden flashes of inspiration. He borrowed his image from Richard Wagner (who, for his part, let himself be prompted to assume Rembrandtian poses and clothing in his portraits).

It is frequently noted with surprise – and held to be so much the more revolutionary – that the first truly noted fashion creator was a man, in a domain that until then had been primarily dominated by women. In fact, however, this lies altogether in the logic of the thing. The role of artist, in the ready-made aura of which Worth fashioned himself, and from whose claim to authenticity he profited, is the male role *par excellence*. Worth ruled like an absolutist prince – at least over the women whom he dominated by the dictates of his genius. For Worth, all women were, by virtue of their sex, the same. On the other hand, since he was exclusively preoccupied with questions of beauty, elegance and appearance, he was not like other men. As the ruler over the powerless, he parodied the role of the absolute ruler. The shadow of the nobility fell on him, and its correlate: unmanliness. Hardly surprising then that doubts arose as to the manliness of the *couturier*. These doubts underlie the consternation expressed in a passage from Dickens, in which the fitting-session appears as the prelude to an act that then fails to ensue: 'Would you believe that in the latter half of the nineteenth century there are bearded milliners, authentic men ... who with their solid fingers, take the exact dimensions of the highest titled women in Paris – robe them, unrobe them and make them turn backward and forward before them?'[32]

It is then precisely not the case, contrary to what is always claimed, that the theory of *l'art pour l'art*, the new type of man represented by the dandy, and the autonomization of fashion were apolitical phenomena. Rather, what they have in common is that they effect a subversion of the modern body politic – of that which, in modernity, the 'political,' whether bourgeois or proletarian, has come to mean – and this means, in the first place, a subversion of the political body. The collective formed on the basis of a shared masculinity seems to be split up and endangered by two factors: the feminine and the noble. In standing apart the dandy refuses the *masculine condition*, that in which all men share by the mere fact of being a man. To the extent that the dandy obviously places the highest value on his clothing – so that he often went broke, even to the point of ruin, for the sake of his appearance – he not only eroticizes his body but also positions himself within the context of pure appearance (*Schein*), a context ideologically foreign to bourgeois, masculine being (*Sein*). The accompanying eroticization thus remains paradoxically under the sign of the feminine.

What is it that structurally happens here? The classifications of male/unmarked/authentic, so central for identity, which is to say, for the opposition of masculine and feminine, are opened up. The dandy, a curiously inauthentic man, makes other men appear less authentically, less naturally masculine. *Haute couture* derives its refinement and wit from just this rupture, from these dissonances. From the beginning of *haute couture*, fashion has been, in the end, nothing less than a form of cross-dressing. At the risk of overstating the case, fashion is masquerade:[33] transvestism, travesty. Its star is, not by chance, the transvestite. Christian Lacroix remarked that his most elegant clients were no

longer women, but New York queens. The woman responsible
for having fundamentally revolutionized European fashion, and
its attendant concept of femininity, presents her work in the
name of the opposite sex: Rei Kawakubo keeps shop under the
name of 'Comme des Garçons.' It would be too easy, however,
to circumscribe fashion as cross-dressing in terms of a simple
exchange, of 'man as woman' or 'woman as man.' In fashion,
gender and class intersect. *Haute couture* dresses women not
simply as normal men, but as dandies.

From its beginnings, *haute couture* has been an adaptation
of the fashion of the dandy for women. It begins by discarding
the feminine article par excellence: Paul Poiret gets rid of the
corset.[34] With his long and extremely tight dresses, which gave
the impression of a certain arabesque figure when worn, Poiret
later prided himself on having deprived women once more,
from below, of the freedom of movement that they had acquired
with the absence of the corset.[35] This sadism, which appeared in
the guise of poetic justice, was calculated to conceal one of his
greatest flops: it was Poiret in fact who had attempted in vain
to introduce European women to the kind of pants worn in the
Orient by both men and women, and thus to introduce not only
total freedom of movement for the legs, but also the masculine
article of clothing par excellence, into women's fashion. Such a
thing had not happened since the French Revolution, when it
was prescribed by decree who wore the pants. The revolutionary
decree, which established the order of the sexes in no uncertain
terms, was declared law in the much celebrated Code Napoléon,
in order to return the 'gendered beings who had gotten out of
control' to their place, and to set an end to their 'most offensive
lack of restraint.'[36] Even the exotic index of orientalism, which
had taken the sting out of the masculine from the very outset
(since the oriental *per se* stood in suspicious proximity to
effeminacy), did not help Poiret and his pants.

The style of the dandy was definitively assimilated into *haute
couture* by Coco Chanel, who facilitated its integration in every
respect. Marlene Dietrich's tuxedo, introduced into *haute couture*
by Yves Saint Laurent in the 1970s, represents the final link in a
long chain of appropriations. Chanel, speaking of herself in the
third person, is said to have confided to Salvador Dali that 'she
took the English masculine and made it feminine. All her life, all
she did was change men's clothing into women's: jackets, hair,

neckties, wrists.'[37] In this way, she invented the New Woman. One easily recognizes that the godfather of this new femininity in the sign of the masculine was not the sexually unmarked, bourgeois man, but the dandy, celebrated by Baudelaire as the Black Prince of elegance. Chanel paid him a lasting homage in opposing her spare and perfect 'little black dress' to Poiret's electric colors with their ostentatious and exotic luxury. That the dandy is the reference becomes apparent, not because of the kind of clothing appropriated, but rather because of the manner in which this fashion is worn. The *désinvolture*, the nonchalance, the poverty *de luxe*, as Poiret indulging in oriental lavishness derisively called it – in short, the carefully cultivated appearance of not having invested any thought into the clothes that one wears – all this belongs to the credo of the perfect dandy.

A different model of the overlapping of class and gender is represented by Dior, when he clothes woman as *femme/femme*, as only woman, as wholly woman at last – which means once again as unscrupulously artificial and hampered – supposedly, in other words, without the detour through the masculine. Interestingly, Coco Chanel interpreted this detour through the masculine as 'naturally' feminine. Chanel herself confidently maintained that she clothed real women for real life. If Chanel dressed woman as dandy, Dior, with his ultra-feminized New Look – wasp waist, corset, full skirt and stiletto heels – did not succeed in transforming his clients into real women – as the relieved press, confronted with such captivating femininity, mistakenly supposed. Chanel, reacting to this new fashion 'like a red flag to a bull, loudly and angrily hissing,' had a better sense of what was going on. She was of the opinion that Dior had dressed his clients up as transvestites. Beside herself with rage, Chanel is supposed – at least according to the reports of her biographers – to have screeched loudly and angrily at two girls who were unfortunate enough to cross her path in their new acquisitions.

> Look at them. Fools dressed by queens living out their fantasies. They dream of being women, so they make real women look like transvestites... They can barely walk. I made clothes for the new woman. She could move and live naturally in my clothes. Now look what those creatures have done. They don't know women. They've never *had* a woman![38]

Ms. Chanel attributed the terrible *faux pas* of 'these creatures' to the fact that a fashion designer such as Dior could not have known what a woman was, since he himself had never had one. We post-Lacanians, as it were, know better: we know that it does not help to have had a woman. Chanel's women – although she was a woman herself and had had women too – were not more natural in the least. They were perhaps more modern, since they embodied not the type of the *femme/femme* but rather that of the *garçonne* – which is something quite different from the natural female.

Chanel is mistaken then, when she stakes her claim to dress the real, natural woman. Fashion has become differentiation from the 'natural' gender, the tension by which the naturalness of gender is unmasked as a fiction. It is like a rhetorical figure which lays bare the claimed naturalness of gender as a rhetorical effect and, at the same time, further displaces it. Chanel's dandy-fashion is the translation of a translation. It is the reappropriation of the prior appropriation of fashion by a small number of men; fashion, under the sign of the feminine and the noble, was to be won back from the men. This new masculinity is transposed by Chanel onto women who now no longer appear natural in their disguise. The disguising of the woman can be highlighted by various means: it can be hyperbolically pronounced and de-naturalized.

The decisive difference which fashion makes lies in this space between the adaptations of the dandy-fashion by *haute couture* and *prêt-à-porter* and the demands of the suffragettes (and also of certain feminist currents) for male clothing. While the suffragettes strive to attain subjectivity through neutralization of gender, and oppose authenticity and the equality of rights to the objectification of women and costumery, the dandy-fashion originated out of a male protest against the same collective, and the identity that is normativized within it: out of a protest which stands under the sign of femininity.

The reform movement in clothing supported by various parts of the suffragette movement attempted to eradicate this evil through a type of clothing that was intended to be 'naturally' attractive to women. This clothing, which sought in the name of the natural to avoid any suggestion of the erotic, was supposed to allow women to dissolve into the collective of men in unmarked sexuality. These efforts were not crowned with success. For it is true here as well that, in an opposition of two terms, the one, here authenticity, remains dependent upon the other, inauthenticity, and both terms function only in and as an oppositional relation. The inauthenticity of women is the necessary condition for the authenticity of men. Formulating itself as a discourse in clothes about clothes, as a kind of commentary, the direction followed by fashion has been the exact opposite of that taken by the reform movement in clothing. Rather than unmarking sexuality, it has marked and overmarked sexuality. On the trail of the vicissitudes of desire, it can do nothing but mark sexuality as paradox. On the one side, it establishes the division of the genders 'feminine'/ 'masculine' – that is to say, marked versus unmarked sexuality, 'inauthentic' versus 'authentic' – by making this division visible; at the same time, however, it disrupts this constitutive opposition. It is self-deconstructive, undermining what it constitutes. And it does so, such is the thesis here, through hyperfetishization. Fashion is a fetishism of the second degree.

The first-degree fetishism of clothing becomes tangible in the female body, which is overstressed in its secondary sexual characteristics. This body is manifest in the roaring success of the wonder and push-up-bra, and the high sales of the bustle or padded girdle. Women are supposed to embody a norm that is simultaneously an ideal form, the schema of an ideal, standard-setting body. If the bustle, when worn by women, is designed to increase their erotic appeal in the eyes of men, when worn by men, it (and other types of padding) serve, according to findings of the magazine *Focus*, less to emphasize their masculine appeal in the eyes of women than their career potential. The padded female body refers to the fashions of the nineteenth century, which went to such extremes in the eroticization of the female body that hats were launched that provided instructions for those able to decipher them as to how the crinoline was to be opened. While the male body almost disappeared beneath loosely fitting fabric, the silhouette of the female body was staged as a production in increasingly surface-intensive and spatially extensive terms.[39] The production of femininity was, and is becoming once more, a full-time job. Between diets, the gym, the hairdresser's, the beauty salon and shopping, the women in Cooker's film *Women* and Woody Allen's film *Alice* have hardly enough time left over to spin their intricate webs of intrigue around a hardly visible and completely inconspicuous husband. The heroine of *Clueless* not only spends exhausting days in the shopping mall; she also puts together her wardrobe by computer, and checks the effect with a video camera. Like Cooker's women before her, she is a heroine of manipulation. As a branch of production, femininity does not remain a privilege of the upper class. On the contrary, it facilitates the possibility of tearing down class distinctions. Frederick's of Hollywood, whose catalogues supplied American women for over twenty years with padding, supports, and bindings of all kinds (see Figure 2), with corsages, satin nightgowns and sexy

Figure 2

Frederick's of Hollywood, 1955.

lace underwear, very early on conceived of this disruption of the structure of class relations – which in French novels tends to appear more as a phenomenon of unrest – in terms of its American democratic potential: they wanted to use sexiness as a means of providing all women with equal opportunity – not in relation to men, of course, but rather in the eyes of men.[40]

Fetishism is in the air; one could almost speak at present of a fetishization of fetishism. If my description of the modern depends upon the fetish, this is because in fashion the fetish arrives at its ancestral realm: the realm of the stuff of which dreams are made, the realm of accessories. The structure that determines the fetish – the oscillation between the animate and the inanimate – is unceasingly staged in fashion. The artificial is naturalized, the natural becomes artificial. Already in its etymological sense of 'making, producing, manufacturing,' the fetish is a product of art, associated with artificiality. The female body must then also count as such a product of art.

If the concept of the fetish is allowed to slip over into the psycho-analytic register, then femininity becomes first and foremost a substitute. It does not refer to itself but rather to man: it stands for his wealth, his power. One recalls the wonderful ambiguity of the wealthy or potent (*vermögend*) man in Freud's analysis of Dora. As Veblen once succinctly put it, the woman exhibits the man's potency. Paradoxically, the ideal femininity embodied in the real woman signifies 'man.' Only man is allowed the privilege of proper meaning, of a literal identity. This is the most profound reason that the feminine gender role is from the very outset a travesty.[41]

Ideal femininity, idealized femininity, femininity as it is supposed to 'be,' is determined by the sign of the masculine, its signified. The difference between the sexes is fixed in a hierarchized opposition, that assigns an unequivocal place to each sex, and thereby secures sexual identity. This arrangement, which secures the principle of identity through the principle of opposition, functions at its core fetishistically: masculinity is complemented and brought to completion in relation to the difference of the sexes, or castration, which is threateningly inscribed within femininity, while castration is distorted and real sexual difference thereby extinguished. The women is ideally consumed in her relation to the masculine. Only insofar as 'she' is mere woman, can he be wholly man. She no longer appears as his mirror image

– as castrated woman – but rather as the fascinating, beguiling object of desire: she 'is' his wealth, his potency. Femininity is thus a masquerade, and his supposed being (*Sein*) is the product of her seeming (*Schein*).

The secret of *haute couture* lies in transvestism, the travesty of this travesty, the masquerade of the masquerade. It thus has an affirmative, hyperfetishistic structure, exhibiting the oppositionally secured, unequivocal identity of sex as the result of masquerade, and toppling literal, unmarked masculinity.[42] 'Exhibition' here means either the marking or cancellation of the fetish that is 'femininity.' Fashion does not represent the sexes; therefore the alternative program to the marked or cancelled fetish of 'femininity' cannot be the true, finally authentic woman. If it represents at all, then fashion represents the unrepresentability of sexual difference, the impossibility, in other words, of not wearing a mask. It does so by completely and recklessly exploiting sexual difference, the oppositionally organized identity of social gender roles. Precisely through this unscrupulous bringing-into-play of the clichés of gender roles, the true woman and the real man emerge as phantasma in a system of the sexes that has been fetishized and phallicized into pure identity. In drag, the gender role that drag is becomes visible to the precise extent that it completely affirms the object of desire, femininity, in its fetishization. Whether metaphor or hyperbole, whether as dandy or as dream woman, it is not possible to dress oneself 'naturally.'[43]

In the 1970s male protest against the male collective emerges in many forms. Young men wear long hair, perfume, make-up, colorful shirts. A general dandyization sets in: a heightened eroticization is aimed for through the denaturalization of the sexes. If earlier the hope was to abandon the limit, and thus the difference between the sexes, now the desire is to play with this limit, the most forbidden of all, to displace it, to disguise it. Its not a matter of identity now, but of difference. The place of this difference is no longer the male as identity-founding principle, but the feminine, as the other of this principle, as the deconstruction of identity. Its *topos* is the fashion of modernity, in which the fetish 'femininity' circulates vertiginously between the sexes.

Woman as dandy, woman as transvestite. In the early days of *haute couture*, woman most certainly embodies the fetish of femininity. This clear relation changes in the fashion of the 1980s, in the era of postfashion. That does not mean that as a result the division between femininity and masculinity has grown less sharp; it has, however, distanced itself ever more from 'natural' gender. Four types emerge in fashion that had not previously existed, making up the four basic possibilities of what I have termed postfashion. First, man can shine forth in the beguiling brilliance of the fetish of femininity: man as man as woman. This fashion very often no longer has anything idealizing about it, as had been the case for instance with Dior's *femme/femme*. Even if in Dior's ultra-femininity the sublime and the ridiculous are, to quote Napoleon, only a step apart, with Dior the scales clearly tip in the direction of sublimity and authentification. This is also true, we note in passing, of other ultra-fetishistic designers, such as Montana, Mugler or Versace. With Gaultier, on the other hand, they move rather in the direction of the ridiculous. The point of reference for his flamboyant drags are no longer the *grande dame*, commanding the attention of everyone around her, nor even the merely charming girl next door, but rather the petit bourgeois woman who, eager to conform, bravely chases after the ideal of the dream woman and is all the more ridiculously helpless for her efforts. Weird and not pretty: such could be Gaultier's motto – and not just his either.

Second, the fetish of feminity, having been appropriated by men, can be stolen and reappropriated – together with the inscribed traces of the first appropriation – by women – without, however, running the risk of authentification or naturalization. Third – and this is probably the most pure and formally refined type of fashion, one that has at times been referred to as deconstruction – woman can carry a fetishized femininity with her as a kind of mask or masquerade, exhibiting herself as a more or less unsuccessful embodiment of 'natural' femininity. Fourth, woman can take on the allure of an injured fetish, in whom the trace of castration has been registered. This mode finds its expression less in clothing than in fashion photography, and is most impressively illustrated by Richardson.

Before I come to Jean-Paul Gaultier, the contemporary designer who perhaps most effectively, if not most subtly, carries out the dismantling of the fetish of femininity through woman, I would like to glance briefly at a Belgian designer from the Antwerp school, Martin Margiela. Margiela does not work primarily with

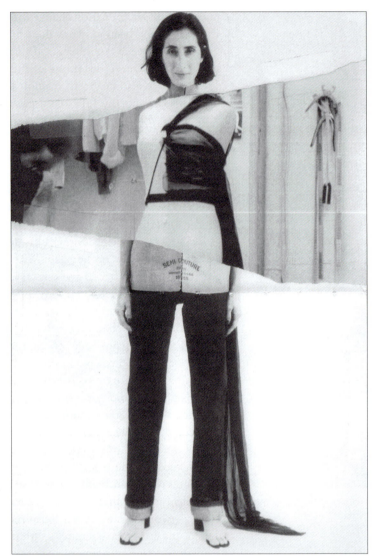

Figure 3
Martin Margiela, 1997, in
La maison Martin Margiela:
(9/4/1615), Museum
Boijman Van Beuningen,
Rotterdam, © Maison
Martin Margiela.

cross-dressing; rather he has developed a strictly formal, and with respect to fashion understood as a coded system, most innovative and radical procedure of exposing the difference between the fetish of femininity and woman (see Figure 3). His fashion makes the body readable as a site of fetishistic inscriptions, precisely because it is not identical to these inscriptions, does not embody them, but rather bears fetishistic femininity as a construct foreign to it. This is achieved through a refined interaction between the tailor's dummy – in French *mannequin* – as the measure by which bodies are normed, and to which all bodies are reduced, and the living body – between tailor's dummy and woman. Margiela pulls the mannequin from out of the 'obscene' beyond and into the spotlight of the stage. He dresses his women as mannequins, as tailor's dummies. His finished clothes look as if they were still on the mannequin, pinned with tacking thread, the modeling pins and threads turned outward, visibly adorned with all the technical accoutrements of production. They expose and turn inside out all the tricks of the tailor's trade that are usually so perfectly concealed. The art of tailoring consists in allowing the body of this dummy, embodied by women, to appear as nature. Named after the tailor's dummy – in Flemish *mannekin* – live mannequins set the dummy's body in motion. The perfect woman, if one follows the Flemish trace at the heart of French fashion, is, in purely etymological terms, a *mannekin*, a little man not so much in the sense of diminution, but in the sense rather of the – detachable – masculine sex: accessory. These 'unfinished' clothes expose the hidden nexus of fashion as fascination with the inanimate, with the dummy or doll. In Margiela's work, this process is exposed and reversed: rather than the inanimate model's being perfectly embodied, the living human body appears as *mannekin*; it appears in the form of a tailor's dummy. Woman is not herself inscribed with the fetish of femininity, but rather this fetish is presented as foreign – as a foreign body.

Gaultier achieves the effect of denaturalization of gender not, like Margiela, through a severely formal procedure immanent to *haute couture* itself, but through a massive staging of fetishized sex. What seems new with Gaultier – and this reflects the sociological fact of a substantial, differentiated and massively prominent homosexual culture – is the fact that fetishized femininity is no longer bound to woman. As queens, fairies and drag queens, men have long appropriated fetishized femininity for themselves. In Gaultier designs, it is evident that the age of renunciation has been left behind. Men's fashion no longer appears in the name of unmarked sexuality, but is instead unscrupulously marked, covered with all the sex symbols available on the market. Like women, Gaultier's men wear furs, bright colors, funky cuts, skin-tight leggings; every form of uniform fetish is indulged. In his winter 1997 fashion show, one could even catch a glimpse of the codpiece, an accessory which I had assumed had definitively run its course. Gaultier deconstructs what had still seemed like the most natural thing in the world in the fashion of Yves Saint Laurent or Versace: namely the idea that woman embodies, and in this embodiment authenticates, fetishized femininity.

On the one hand, man now becomes the privileged bearer of fetishized femininity and men's fashion becomes absolutely flamboyant. On the other hand, woman wears the fetish of femininity as a foreign body periodically disrupted by masculine appropriation. Particularly appropriate in this respect is Gaultier's response to the Kunigunde-like sex symbols of a Frederick's of Hollywood.[44] While the latter naturalized the fetishized feminine, Gaultier literally turned inside out the process by which the woman inhabits fetishized femininity. Bustle and bra, garter belt and corset are worn on top of the dress. Yet another version of this displacement of fetishized femininity can be seen in Vivienne Westwood's 1995 winter collection, dedicated to the cocotte and her aggressive, exaggerated eroticism. It was not only the complicated *décolletés* in corsages that modeled the breasts according to all the tricks of the trade, adorned with oversized bows, which were impressive: lifted by the bustle, the *derrière* presented itself charmingly, if in an exaggerated fashion. This displacement of the feminine was driven a step further in the 1997 summer collection *Angels* of Comme des Garçons, to the point where displacement threatened to slip into disfigurement. Yunja Watanabe, the only designer of Comme des Garçons who signs his own line, made his debut by literally displacing femininity. The bra pads were situated on the back, the bustle clearly shifted around on to the thigh. This displaced and thereby emphasized femininity had a point that was more than just ironic or parodic. The truly novel silhouette oscillated between a misshapen figure reminiscent of the hunchback of Notre Dame, and a completely unexpected and new gracefulness that had definitively abandoned the harmonious symmetry of classical statuary as the measure for Western perfection. Thus with its 1997 summer collection Comme des Garçons succeeded in achieving the truly unexpected and unheard of: the creation of a new silhouette out of the displacement of an old and reupholstered femininity. Like an angel; not quite of this world?

When Dior or even Saint Laurent dress women as drag queens, this process is hidden and naturalized. Women are supposed to be able to embody fetishized femininity perfectly – real to the feel, as it were. Gaultier, however, introduces the traces and loose ends of drag into his clothing, interrupting the process of embodiment by woman, and marking the detour through the masculine body and its distinguishing traits. The most striking example of expropriation and reappropriation in this increasingly vertiginous and meandering circulation of fetishized femininity is the black wool hair, suggestive of masculine chest hair, trimming the *decolleté* of a dress in Gaultier's winter collection of 1993. And even this hair is doubly encoded and ambiguous. For it can refer just as well to the masculine chest *toupée* – an essential element of perfected masculinity – as to natural chest hair, which, having been forgotten or overlooked by drag queens, often provides an unintended trim to an otherwise stunningly 'feminine' *decolleté*. In Gaultier's 1995/6 winter collection man appears as woman as man, thus reappropriating the initial feminine appropriation of the dandy fashion. And so the dizzying circulation of fetishized femininity in the fashion after the fashion has come full circle.

The marking of the marking that femininity is does not have to lead to distortion. The summer collection of 1999 of Yamamoto and Dries Van Noten shows that it can be done with a lighter touch, the elegance of the *belle époque* passing revue in company with *cul de Paris* and crinoline. Yamamoto reveals the production of the padded feminine silhouette as a conjuring trick. It no longer has anything stiff or formal about it; rather, it is light, portable, inflatable, detachable. Yamamoto's hoop-skirts, for example, are not lined with whalebone but with inflatable, lustrous black padding, which can also be worn without the skirt covering it. The crinoline effect is achieved by wafer-thin constructions under black stretch-fabric. Most of these creations, like those of Watanabe, can also be transformed from two-dimensional to three-dimensional objects. Dries Van Noten achieved his *cul de Paris* by transporting the secrets of rustic Europe through the additions of a few buttons and gathers. The body is displayed as an art object, the possibility of its being modeled and shaped openly exhibited.

In the 1980s, there also appears a new discourse on fashion, confirming the phenomenon that, nurtured with art and the dandy, now emerges from its long latency. With Paul Yonnet, fashion becomes the vehicle of a revolution from above, in which an elite individualism, that of the *individu roi*, slowly filters down.[45]

In this revolution, the feminine stands against the totalitarian forms and dangers of modern democracy, civilization stands against politics, the individual stands against the stereotypes of mass culture, and the competition of appearances stands against the uniformization and collectivization which the disaster of the world wars had made possible. *Haute couture* will no longer be seen as left over from the time of the nobility, a relic of a past epoch. With it, comes the moment of a new individualism, of the affirmation of asocial modes of conduct. This individual does not stand above society (as does the individual of Simmel), but rather against it, against the form of the Republic which we, in our modern states, whether communist–socialist or democratic, have inherited from Rousseau, and which has its being in the mystically unified body of the general will. This new individual stands in the sign of appearance, of the asocial abandon of luxury, in short, in the name of the eternally destructive arch-enemy of the mystical manly body of the modern Republic – the feminine. The new look had announced itself, for Yonnet, in the 'Zazous,' a phenomenon dating from the time of the German occupation of France. At this time too, certain young men had nothing better to do than to occupy themselves with their look, to the general indignation: to let their hair grow, and in a time of the most severe rationing of leather, to acquire as much leather as possible through shady transactions on the black market in order to be up with the latest fashion, which made leather plateau-soles into an absolute must. They drew upon themselves the hatred of all politically correct thinkers of the time: that of the Resistance, for their lack of political seriousness, that of the French province for their effeminate luxury.

Gilles Lipovetsky largely follows Yonnet's tendency, with some humanist deradicalization. For him too, fashion has become the dominant phenomenon, the signature of post-ideological society, of society at the end of the twentieth century as a *société-mode*.[46] This would be the culmination of democracies that have shed their ideologically doctrinaire character. For Lipovetsky, as for Yonnet, this is no ideal condition, but rather the lesser evil in a Europe that has torn itself apart for centuries in murderous wars of ideology. Having represented the nostalgia of noble life forms and the concretization of an imagined femininity, fashion has now taken on the allure of a way out, through which it becomes the last and most literal embodiment of its European past. What fashion embodies is, according to its belated philosophical spokesman, 'individuality' – but individuality in the sign of appearance rather than of being: no longer – according to the thesis I would like to advance here – individuality in the sense of manly identity, but rather in the sense of feminine difference. In the 1980s, more or less simultaneously with its philosophical discovery, this after-image of the old European spirit passes through a number of decisive modifications. It gains a new lease of life. This is what I would like to refer to as postfashion.

With the 1970s, the fashion of a hundred years, the continuous line stretching from Worth to Saint Laurent, comes to an end. In Schiaperelli and Chanel, it found its high point as a fashion of modernity. The Paris show of Comme des Garçons, in 1981, spectacularly marked the end of one era and the beginning of another. The firm of the Japanese designer Rei Kawakubo presents itself under a name which encapsulates the transition perfectly: what it suppresses for a change is the name of the designer. The creative impulses now come from *prêt-à-porter*, and not from *haute couture*. Postfashion breaks the dominance of Paris fashion, which with its couturiers had been the last remainder of French power of the eighteenth century. Above all, it breaks the dictatorial privilege of the great couturiers. The fashion designer loses his absolute power. His inspirations no longer come to him from an obscure genius. Fashion becomes a co-production between the *créateur* and those who wear the clothes. Whether fashion is interesting is no longer dependent on the designer alone, but in equal part, on people in the street: on what they 'make' out of what is on offer, as Yohji Yamamoto says. But this is only one possible formulation, somewhat adapted to the style of American populism, of what takes place.

Postfashion here means what comes after the completion of the 'hundred-year fashion,' as its after-image. After this fashion, after the great period of *haute couture*, whose image is so vividly elevated to programmatic status by Yonnet and Lipovetsky, there follows a decade, and longer, in which fashion praxis – quite apart from the programmatic potential various post-modernisms will attribute to it – deconstructs modernity and, in the end, leaves it behind. If, for a hundred years, fashion has invented and reinvented 'woman,' postfashion has begun to deconstruct this 'woman.' Where fashion used to disguise its art, it now exhibits its artificiality. In the sign of the old, the used, it prescribes itself an aesthetic of poverty and ugliness, of sentimentality and out-modedness, of kitsch and bad taste, in which elements of the petit bourgeois enter into competition with the outsiders of society. Its heroes are bag ladies and the homeless, but also fragmentary citations from the workers and prostitutes of the older modern, from Baudelaire to Brecht, circus performers and other artists of disguise, nuns and children. Jean-Paul Gaultier like Nina Hagen must have read Pippi Langstrumpf. The solitary star of the new fashion, however, is the transvestite. *La mode de cent ans* now becomes the epitome of the unmodern, its class and gender stereotypes the ceaseless target of the citations and displacements of its successors.

Notes

1. See Mark C. Taylor, *Hiding*, Chicago 1997, p. 169.
2. Thorstein Veblen, *The Theory of the Leisure Class – An Economic Study of Institutions*, New York 1919, p. 182.
3. See Pierre Bourdieu, *Distinction: A Social Critique of the Judgment of Taste*, trans. Richard Nice, Cambridge, MA 1989.
4. Veblen, *The Theory of the Leisure Class*, p. 182.
5. Ibid., pp. 183–4
6. Simone de Beauvoir, *Le deuxième sexe*, vol. 2, Paris 1949, p. 206.
7. Karl Marx, *Der achtzehnte Brumaire des Louis Bonaparte*, with an introduction by Friedrich Engels, ed. D. Rjazanov, Vienna, Berlin 1927, p. 21.
8. Ibid., p. 127.
9. Giacomo Leopardi, who, in his *Dialogo della Moda e della Morte*, seems to pursue a similar vein, undercuts this moral condemnation since it is Mme Mort herself who is contaminated by her 'sister' Madame Mode and becomes fashionable herself. In *Operette Morali*, Milan 1999 (1824).
10. Erika Thiel, *Geschichte des Kostüms*, East Berlin 1980, p. 208.

11. Charles Secondat Baron de Montesquieu, *The Spirit of Laws*, Book XIX, Chap. 8, in *Encyclopedia Britannica*, ed. William Benton, Chicago 1952, p. 136.
12. Montesquieu, *The Spirit of Laws*, Book VII, Chap. 9, p. 47.
13. Jean-Jacques Rousseau, *Politics and the Arts – Letter to M. D'Alembert on the Theatre*, trans. with notes and an introduction by Allan Bloom, Ithaca 1987, p. 100.
14. Rousseau, *Politics and the Arts*, p. 112.
15. Honoré de Balzac, *Physiologie de la toilette*, in *Traité des excitants modernes; suivi de Physiologie de la toilette; et de Physiologie gastronomique*, with a preface by Jean-Jacques Brochier, Bègles 1992.
16. Anne Hollander, in one of her most recent books *Sex and Suits: The Evolution of Modern Dress*, New York 1995 has attempted to free fashion from this stigma of femininity. She inscribes herself thereby explicitly in the line of the moderns, who oppose function to ornament: the basic opposition belongs together with a whole series of oppositions which shape the theory of fashion. 'Modern' thought opposes depth to superficiality, seriousness to frivolity, naturalness to artificiality, reason to sensuality, and above all, of course, masculinity to femininity. For a very explicit example, one can turn to Adolf Loos, *Spoken into the Void: Collected Essays 1897–1900*, trans. Jane Newman and John Smith, Cambridge 1982. Hollander's argument for fashion takes over all the arguments which the discourse of art and architecture had used, following in the Rousseauist tradition, to distinguish their own domains from that of fashion. Hollander seeks to disengage fashion from the grip of post-modernism and gender-confusion, and thus to turn it into a serious subject. The development of fashion therefore is seen as running parallel to that of modern art and architecture: it consists in a movement beyond the feminine and ornamental, and, concretely, beyond the milliner. It is driven forward by the tailor, who develops a functional cutting-technique, leading to the modern men's suit. This suit, Hollander claims enthusiastically, gives to every man not only the classical beauty of an Apollo of Belvedere and the aura of sovereign power, but also the sexiness of a predatory tiger. If the women of the nineteenth century limp somewhat behind the blessing of this suit, at once so practical and so beautiful,

so comfortable and so sexy, nonetheless, in the twentieth century, they gradually come to appreciate the pleasures of the modern, masculine tendency, which leaves all superficiality, all the fussy little ornamental bits and pieces behind. See Mark C. Taylor, 'De-signing,' in: *Hiding*, pp. 167–217. But then, of course, even this antifashion is part of fashion as you can see in 'clean' designers, mostly American, such as Calvin Klein, to give but one example. On the problem of Mannerism and classicism, see in particular Ursula Link-Heer, 'Die Mode im Museum oder Manier und Stil (mit einem Blick auf Versace),' in *Mode, Weiblichkeit und Modernität*, ed. Gertrud Lehnert, Dortmund 1998, pp. 140–64.

17. J.C. Flugel, *The Psychology of Clothes*, London 1930, pp. 110ff.

18. Gabriele Mentges, 'Der Mensch nach Maß – der vermessene Mensch,' in *Moden und Menschen*, Stuttgart 1995, p. 42.

19. Richard Alewyn and Karl Sälzle, *Das große Welttheater – Die Epoche der höfischen Feste in Dokument und Deutung*, Hamburg 1959, p. 36.

20. See as the most telling example Chodowiecki: Ingrid Sommer (ed.), *Der Fortgang der Tugend und des Lasters: Daniel Chodowieckis Monatskupfer zum Göttinger Taschenkalender mit Erklärungen Georg Christoph Lichtenbergs 1778–1783*, Berlin 1974.

21. Jacques Lacan, 'The Meaning of the Phallus,' in *Feminine Sexuality – Jacques Lacan and the école freudienne*, ed. Juliet Mitchell and Jacqueline Rose, New York 1985, pp. 74–85.

22. Bernard Mandeville, *The Fable of the Bees: Or, Private Vices, Publick Benefits*, with a commentary by F.B. Kaye, Oxford 1924.

23. Georg Simmel, 'Die Mode,' in *Philosophische Kultur*, Leipzig 1919, p. 44.

24. Simmel, 'Die Mode,' p. 32.

25. René König, *Macht und Reiz der Mode*, Vienna, Düsseldorf 1971, pp. 125–7.

26. Rudolph von Ihering, *Der Zweck im Recht II*, Leipzig 1883, cited by Walter Benjamin, *The Arcades Project*, vol. 1 (Convolut B 'Fashion'), trans. Howard Eiland and Kevin McLaughlin, Cambridge 1999, p. 75.

27. Ibid.

28. Egon Friedell, *Kulturgeschichte der Neuzeit III*, Munich 1931, p. 203, cited by Benjamin, *The Arcades Project*, p. 75.

29. Simmel, 'Die Mode,' pp. 25–7.
30. Thomas Meinecke, *Tomboy*, Frankfurt 1998, and Chuck Palahniuk, *Invisible Monsters*, New York 1999.
31. Sima Godfrey, 'Haute Couture and Haute Culture,' in *A New History of French Literature*, ed. Dennis Hollier, Cambridge MA 1989, p. 768.
32. Charles Dickens, *All the Year Round* (28 February 1863), p. 9, cited by Valerie Steele, *Women of Fashion – Twentieth-Century Designers*, New York 1991, p. 24.
33. See, for the concept of masquerade, Lacan, 'The Meaning of the Phallus,' pp. 74–85, and Joan Rivière, 'Womanliness as Mascarade,' in *International Journal of Psychoanalysis*, X, 1929, pp. 303–13. For recent discussions of the concept see *Weiblichkeit als Maskerade*, ed. Liliane Weissberg, Frankfurt 1995, and *Maskeraden – Geschlechterdifferenz in der literarischen Inszenierung*, eds Elfi Bettinger and Julika Funk, Berlin 1995.
34. For the endless discussion on the corset see Valerie Steele, *The Corset: A Cultural History*, New Haven 2001.
35. Paul Poiret, *En habillant l'époque*, Paris 1974 (1930); quoted in Paul Yonnet, *Jeux, modes et masses*, Paris 1986, p. 320.
36. Gundula Wolter, 'Lieber sterb' ich, als meiner Frau die Hose zu lassen: Zur Kulturgeschichte der Frauenhose,' in *Moden und Menschen*, Stuttgart 1995, p. 72.
37. André Parinaud, *The Unspeakable Confession of Salvador Dali*, New York 1981, p. 212, cited by Steele, *Women of Fashion*, p. 41.
38. Franco Zeffirelli, *Zeffirelli – An Autobiography*, New York 1986, p. 100, cited by Steele, *Women of Fashion*, p. 50.
39. Robert Musil, *Die Frau gestern und morgen* (1929), in *Gesammelte Werke*, vol. 8, Hamburg 1978, pp. 1193–8.
40. Laura and Janusz Gottwald, *Frederick's of Hollywood 1947–73 – 26 Years of Mail Order Seduction*, New York 1970, p. 9.
41. Shoshana Felman, 'Rereading Femininity,' in *Yale French Studies* 62 (1981), 19–44.
42. Zeffirelli, *An Autobiography*, p. 100.
43. Judith Butler, *Gender Trouble. Feminism and the Subversion of Identity*, New York 1990.
44. In Heinrich von Kleist's *Käthchen von Heilbronn*, Kunigunde is the aristocratic bride, a mosaique work, with false teeth, hair, breasts and waist, who takes off the components of her

seductive femininity every evening, and lays them on a chair for the morning. She is thus a deceitful replication of Helen of Troy, the artifice of femininity itself.

45. Yonnet, *Yeux, modes et masses*.
46. Gilles Lipovetsky, *L'empire de l'éphémère – La mode et son destin dans les sociétés modernes*, Paris 1987.

2

Adorned in Zeitgeist

Fashion has become what art had wanted to be: the *Zeitgeist* expressing itself in visible form. Its stage is no longer the aristocratic salon or the gatherings of select society at the theater, opera or racecourse. Fashion is now made, worn and displayed, not by the bourgeoisie or the aristocracy, but on the street. The great cities – London, Berlin, New York, Paris, Tokyo, Rome – are the *theatrum mundi* on which it makes its entrance. Baudelaire's irresistible passerby, carried by the crowd, with a flourish of seam and frill, past the spectator-poet, his red-haired beggar woman, craving cheap costume jewelry, are early symptoms of this change of scene.[1] They indicate a new relation of beauty and ideal, one which continues to exercise a latent effect until the end of the following century.

Walter Benjamin remarks somewhat offhandedly in one of the entries in his *Arcades Project* that the eternal is far more the ruffle on a dress than some idea.[2] The assertion is provocative and looks, at first glance, absurd: is not the frill on the dress the frivolous emblem of futility, of the arbitrary and ever-changing whims of fashion? Fashion, the empire of the ephemeral, is the very antithesis of the profundity and serene beauty of ideas. The time of fashion is not eternity, but the moment. Coco Chanel defines the art of the designer as 'l'art de capter l'air du temps.' Paul Morand, her ghostwriter and friend, compared it for that reason to Nemesis, the goddess of destruction: it lives from destruction, not only that of the preceding fashion, but also from its own extinction: 'The more ephemeral fashion is, the more perfect it is. You can't protect what is already dead.'[3] Fashion is defined as the art of the perfect moment, of the sudden, surprising and yet obscurely expected harmonious apparition – the Now at the threshold of an immediate future. But its realization is, at the same time, its destruction. By appearing, and giving definitive form to the moment, fashion is almost already part of yesterday. Courrèges's immaculate very young girl, a modern, minimalist virgin, lean, clad in white, and waiting for things to come, is a perfect allegory of fashion. For the same reason, perhaps, fashion shows traditionally end with the veiled bride, a figure of great expectations. Fashion is the moment that negates time as *durée*; it erases the traces of time, blots out history as difference by positioning itself as absolute, self-evident and perfect as a moment becoming eternity, the promise of eternity. The veil of melancholy only heightens the poignant beauty of the fleeting moment, its ephemerality and frailness.

Benjamin's almost too quotable paradox alludes to, and even quotes from, Baudelaire's *Tableaux parisiens*, from the sonnet dedicated 'A une passante.' Its heroine is not a bride clad in white expectancy, but a widow dressed in the funereal elegance of black mourning. The contrast of transitory moment and eternity is the crucial opposition structuring the poem; 'un éclair, puis la nuit': a fugitive beauty revealed in a flash-like revelation.[4] Before the ecstatic meeting of the gazes, before he looks into her eyes (in which a storm is announced), a statuesque leg shows forth from under the swaying frill, the delicately balanced skirt seam.

> *Beauté fugitive*
> *Dont le regard m'a fait soudainement renaître*
> *Ne te verrai-je plus que dans l'éternité?*

The frill came into play some lines before:

Longue, mince, en grand deuil, douleur majestueuse
Une femme passa, d'une main fastueuse
Soulevant, balançant le feston et l'ourlet.

The deafening street was screaming all around me.
Tall, slender, in deep mourning – majestic grief –
A woman made her way, with fastidious hand
Raising and swaying festoon and hem;

Agile and noble, with her statue's limbs.
And there was I, who drank, contorted like a madman,
Within her eyes – that livid sky where hurricane is born –
Gentleness that fascinates, pleasure that kills.

A lightning-flash ... then night! – O fleeting beauty
Whose glance all of a sudden gave me new birth,
Shall I see you again only in eternity?

Far, far from here! Too late! or maybe *never*?
For I know not where you flee, you know not where I go,
O you I would have loved (o you who knew it too!)[5]

Fashion here appears to be incapable of its traditional task towards time: it seems unable to erase history as difference, unable
to leave time behind in the perfection of the Now. Antiquity
lurks under the veil of modernity, death raises its head in the
midst of life, Eros and Thanatos meet. Instead of harmony, a
violent friction is produced. The ephemeral cannot pose as the
eternal. Time and death have left their 'stigmata': with the help
of Proust's *Recherche*, Benjamin reads the symptoms of city life
on the 'passante's' face.

Heinrich Heine was the first to take fashion as the paradigm
of the modern, following the etymological suggestion linking *la
mode* and *la modernité* in French, as well as *Mode* and *Moderne*
in German. Fashion as the ephemeral is the quintessential mo-
mentum of modernity. The ancient and the modern, the eternal
and the ephemeral are no longer antithetical but mutually affect
each other; antiquity, we might say, is no longer safe. This new
relation can be represented as a disfiguration of the eternal, ideal
beauty of the statue by the fashion of the moment. The technical
term for this kind of clash between high and low, as a poetic
genre, is travesty.

Heine wished he could give all the velvet and silk of Solomon to the poor city-girl of southern Trent to underline her antique beauty. But it is the contrast between the eternal ideal of the antique statues and the transitory contemporary beauty, between the classical norms and the cheaply fashionable, with its almost grotesque particularity, the contradiction between the lively hips and the banality of a brown-striped cotton skirt that evokes the most powerful and ambivalent reaction in Heine. With a deep and comical sigh, Heine deplores the travesty and disfiguration of the ideal of classical beauty through the fashion of the times.

Therefore there is many a touching contrast between body and garment; the exquisitely carved mouth seems formed to command, and is itself scornfully overshadowed by a wretched hat with crumpled paper flowers, the proudest breasts heave and palpitate in a frizzle of coarse woollen imitation lace, and the most spiritual hips are embraced by the stupidest cotton. Sorrow, thy name is cotton – and brown-striped cotton at that! For, alas, nothing produced in me such sorrowful feelings as the sight of a fair Trent girl, who in form and complexion resembled a marble goddess, and who wore on this antique noble form a garment of brown-striped cotton, so that it seemed as though the petrified Niobe had suddenly become merry, and disguised herself in our modern small-souled garb, and now swept in beggarly pride and grandiose awkwardness through the streets of Trent.[6]

Like Heine, Baudelaire develops the new aesthetics through the juxtaposition of fashion and statue. 'A une passante' portrays the animation of a statue by fashionable clothing. Fashion does not embody the ideal, but stands rather in a peculiar relation of tension to it. Something new comes out of this clash, a third term, if only a negative one. The new look born from this violent confrontation is romantic irony. Its charm is precisely the harsh, abrupt disruption of tone, the disharmonic, wild and incongruous mixture of high and low, of the ridiculous and the sublime. Romantic irony is this hiatus and thus the decomposition of the eternal beauty of the classical statue and the perfect moment of fashion.

Baudelaire sees fashion no longer in the sign of short-livedness and arbitrary change, but in a lasting tension to the classical incarnation of beauty, to the timeless statues of antiquity. From this tension desire results. Baudelaire's 'passante' is a manifesto of this new style, exposing in passing the grotesque contrast of the sharply disharmonious moment of fashion, a moment that continues barely to escape what it vainly seeks to exclude: the 'differential of time,' as Benjamin has called it. Life and death, mourning and eroticism, antiquity and modernity, eternity and the fleeting moment appear in a reciprocal illumination, in a light that is decidedly not that of ideality.

As the embodiment of the normative, eternal canon of beauty, which it reveals through its sheer geometrical measures, the statue is superhuman, a reflection of the beauty of the gods. The appropriate reaction on the part of the beholder is awe and disinterested admiration. In romanticism, the statue becomes the emblem around which desire is organized – think of Gautier, Barbey d'Aurevilly, James, Hawthorne, or Sacher-Masoch. It is precisely the absence of desire in the statue, the cold white perfection of her marble limbs that inflames desire for her. The stigmata Christianity leaves on antiquity is the conditioning of male sexuality as sadistic, as the desire to stain the immaculate. The uncanny other of the statue, its dark reverse, is the doll. As one sees in E.T.A. Hoffmann's 'Sandmann,' the doll's beauty does not refer to divine beauty, but to the deceiving mechanics of men. Fashion plays with the appeal of statue and doll, with an odd coupling of life and death, life-like appearance. In the apparition of Baudelaire's statuesque women, there is more than a hint of *corps morcelé* and fetishism. Benjamin sees fashion as the very topos of fetishism, as the place of oscillation between the inorganic (such as the statue, for example) and the living. 'Every fashion couples the living body to the inorganic world. Fashion claims the rights of the corpse in the living. Fetishism, based on the sex appeal of the inorganic, is its vital nerve.'[7] The inorganic comes to life – but does not have to bear the stigmata of life, decline and death. Fashion becomes the site at which the ideal can awake to life, hard, white, flawless, complete, eternal like marble, the site at which the mortality of the flesh can be denied. Since woman, as able to give birth, has the more manifest relation to time, i.e. to death, it is she who more insistently requires this transformation. This affinity casts light on the ideal of androgyny as well as on the fascination of sterility. Fashion exhibits the structure which Freud described as 'denial,' and which is characteristic for every fetishism: 'I know, but all the same…'

The white beauty and majesty of antique marble and modern fashion oscillate between the animate and the inanimate: between a statue coming alive, Pygmalion-like, and a living woman becoming an inanimate statue. Her looks kill, but they also lead to rebirth, to a renaissance. The erotic charge of the moment is eternalized, a kind of *piccol' morte*: 'love not at first, but at last sight,' in Benjamin's famous words.[8] The price to pay for this eternalization is the travesty of the sonnet by disjunction, juxtaposition, and decomposition. The serenity of endless blue sky, the blue and white suffused with light that lets this statue appear, is exchanged for the roaring, deafening street in the capital of modernity that carries the 'passante' along with the masses. The erotic nervousness and wantonness of the waving of the frill stand in sharp disharmony, not only to the mourning of the widow, but also to the imperturbability of the statuesque beauty, through which she represents a perfection beyond desire. Instead of the enraptured, sublimated, metaphysical admiration of the once perfect beauty, there is a strange love scene *à l'antique*, with the roles reversed. It is the eyes of the woman that now have the power of Jupiter's thunder and lightning: 'ciel livide où germe l'ouragan.' The lightning that strikes the eye of the beholder with the violence of a sudden blow – 'un éclair, puis la nuit' – alludes to the overwhelming essence of Jupiter, who had to change form so as not to reduce his object of desire to ashes, like Semele. Here the lightning strikes the poet's lyrical persona through the eyes of the obscure object of his desire; he is shaken in sexual rapture and extreme erotic tension – 'crispé comme un extravagant' – as if zapped by an electric shock. This 'crispement,' however, is not merely the particular reaction of an individual, but part of the code of the elegant man, as characterized by Taxile Delord in the Paris-Viveur and described by Benjamin: 'The face of an elegant man should always have … something irritated and convulsive about it. One can attribute this facial agitations either to a natural Satanism, to the fever of passions, or finally to anything one likes.'[9]

Through the description of one of the most typical and common instances of modern city life – the exchange of an erotically charged glance between perfect strangers, representatives of fashionable types rather than individuals – Baudelaire rewrites the history of love poetry, traces the shape of desire in modernity, and indicates the structure of the new fashion. A fleeting moment, *en passant*, that one forgets. If this 'passante' is unforgettable, it is because the poem reproduces, in negative, the aura of a tradition through the shock. Disfigurement produces the trace of the figure. 'The differential of time, in which the dialectical image alone is true, is unknown to Baudelaire,' Benjamin wrote. 'Try to show it through fashion.' 'A une passante,' however, produces this image, and precisely, in a differential of time.[10] In the moment that separates the flash-like appearance of fashion and the eternity of the statue, through the clash of two modes that both negate time, history appears as difference. What appears is not the full history, but the disfiguration modernity produces in antiquity and, at the same time, that which antiquity produces in modernity. The 'passante' in mourning wears the stigmata of time and death. The juxtaposition of times produces the aura in the one and only way it can be produced: as a lost moment. The timeless perfect ideal appears only through the refracted element of its disfiguration.

Although this moment is one of the most erotic in European literature, it is not the erotic attraction which triggers the particular 'shock' of the lyric. Rather, it lies in the sudden knowledge of the desire which is exposed in this moment. For a moment, modern desire shows itself without the veil of ideality: as a desire for inanimate perfection, for that which stands outside time, mortality and decline.

The emblem of such coupling, hidden in the fashion designer's atelier, is the 'mannequin,' the puppet upon which the dresses are modeled. Baudelaire's 'passante' reveals the figure of the antique statue preserved and concealed at the center of fashion, in the guise of the mannequin. In the living mannequin (i.e. the model) – that is, in the animation of the dead puppet-figure – the relation between mannequin and statue becomes thematic; the torso of the statue becomes visible as the model of the model. Hence, it is that the torso becomes the privileged object of modern sculpture and of modern desire. 'This is my feminine ideal: a virgin with no legs to leave me, no arms to hold me, no head to talk to me': thus the sculptor Gordon explains his marble torso in Faulkner's novel *Mosquitoes*.[11] Faulkner here exposes what otherwise remains, and has to remain, carefully veiled over, in order to exercice its attraction – veiled like the bride at the end of every fashion show. If fashion, in its constant alternation, sometimes gives the impression of a fatal monotony, an endless return of the same, this may be because its function is to disguise the fetishistic core of desire in ever new forms. This fetishistic core – fetish as the soul of fashion, or its complete soullessness – is laid bare in postfashion. Here the inherent fetishism of fashion is negotiated in a new way; in one sense, it is entirely in accordance with fashion, in another sense, it goes against the grain of fashion's secret.

The new beauty uncovered by Baudelaire draws on a pot-pourri of historical ideals of beauty. Such is the treasury of junk from which fetishes emerge. His 'red-haired beggar-woman' stands before the background of the women idolized by the poets of the Pléiade: this is where he finds the brilliance of her pearls and diamonds, the velvet and the silk which envelop her, the exquisite fragrances which surround her, the poise of her foot in a charming slipper and, not least, the poems that celebrate her beauty. She was the object of all desires, absolutely sovereign. Baudelaire's poem invokes this past ideal: the modern beggar of the metropolis appears in the rhythm and the verse measure of the Pléiade. With white freckled skin, in her laddered stockings, coarse shoes, the short rags whose ill-tied knots reveal a glimpse of the gleaming beauty of her breasts, she concedes nothing, in the end, to her splendidly attired Renaissance prototype.

The point here, however, is not that the body of the beggar-woman, the sheer materiality of the flesh, is just as beautiful, tempting and seductive as the poetically praised lady of the court: nor even that it would be a pity not to profit from the opportunity. Baudelaire's novelty has nothing to do with the *gaulois* macho naturalism of a Georges Brassens. This unprejudiced character was not ashamed to remove the wooden shoes and coarse woolen stockings of a Helen already scorned by three gentlemen of better society, and was rewarded with 'legs of a princess.'[12] The eye of the connoisseur, according to the facile argument, is not deceived by the outer covering, it goes straight to the essential, to the beauty of the naked female body, independent of class and of class-conditioned fashion. The eroticism of the beggar-woman in Baudelaire is of an entirely different nature. It is not a matter of the physique that has been grievously overlooked: it is rather a metaphysical erotic, beyond physical norms and health, proceeding from a discrepancy of ideal beauty and poverty, from the fact that she has nothing. Her freckles are the mark of a deficiency, announcing a beauty of another kind.

What is absent from Baudelaire's poem is the male hero, the hero who, with the regularity of an amen in the church, responds to the distress of princesses of nineteenth-century novels. There is no charming prince in sight. The poet himself is weak and wretched, and cannot transform the beauty that he sees in this sickly body into a princess. But the bourgeois client, looking for consequence-free sexuality at an excellent price, is also absent. Love, which in the bourgeois period stands under the sign of commerce – in marriage as in prostitution – stands in the aristocratic period under the sign of the gift. Men lavish poetry and jewelry, create, gild, and watch over their ideal. Their ideal holds them under her spell, and, according to her will, generously dispenses or withholds a favor on which they can by no means reckon.

The modern poet, however, has no gift to give. He cannot even buy his beggar-girl the inexpensive costume jewelry that she wants. His poetry, like this jewelry, is cheap. Like a tired remake, he compares, for the hundred-thousandth time, the radiance of breasts with the radiance of eyes. The new ideal is not here the affirmation of the old. On the contrary, the ideal, when it is transposed into this new form, is exhausted, and thus well-matched to the no longer idolized addressee.

The poet is linked to the beggar by his wretchedness, in a solidarity of impotence. They are the same. If he has an advantage, this lies at most in the corrosive self-irony with which he acknowledges that an ideal cannot be regained by imitation, that, on the contrary, it is destroyed by imitation. The moderns, if they do not wish to slip into facile ideology, can only give expression to their desire for ideality in order to deconstruct it. Baudelaire's poem, like postfashion, which can invoke Baudelaire with more justice than most of his successors, shows how much more this means than mere destruction. The new beauty is a beauty in the sign of death, of mourning, of poverty, in the sign of covetousness, of a price, of thin nakedness; it profiles itself before the background of an ideal now disfigured. In a grimace, the form of the Renaissance is distorted, the high style is degraded. The poet's gaze, falling on the beggar, makes her into an equally ridiculous sister in suffering, a mirror of his desire no less than of his impotence.

Baudelaire's poem reflects the process of imitation in the structure of that which is imitated. The later fashion jewelry of Chanel is a suitable emblem for this. In the revaluation of all imitated values, imitation itself does not remain innocent. The genuine appears out of date, the original ridiculous. Fake fur devalues real fur, costume jewelry devalues real jewelry. The surplus value created in the process of devaluation reflects back on the one who recognizes it – as the only possible knowledge value. The fashion of the twentieth century is decisively determined by this figure, of which the poetic praxis of Baudelaire more than later theory of fashion gives us a notion. In the fashion of the 1980s, after one hundred years of the fashion that follows Baudelaire and Mallarmé, the figure suddenly becomes contemporary again. 'Investment' – financial as well as spiritual: the economy of the meanings invested in fashion is the theme of postfashion; 'Geist und Kleid,' an obsessive rhyme of the old Brentano, is the leitmotiv whose figures it plays through. Its play presents the masquerade which makes 'man' and 'woman' into the *dramatis personae* of public life.

Paris is Burning: Femininity as Masquerade

idole, elle doit se dorer pour être adorée

Baudelaire, *Eloge du maquillage*

The title of Jenny Livingston's cult film, *Paris is Burning*, a documentary about black and Latin American men in Harlem who would like to be women, alludes to the displacement that characterizes the entire film: Paris, the distant city of cities, city of luxury, of fashion and beautiful women, is the phantom pursued in Harlem, the New York ghetto and slum, the district of poverty, fear and homosexuality. The connection is forged between Paris and the enclave of northern Manhattan through the medium of fashion. The brilliant displays of the great names like Yves Saint Laurent, Valentino and Chanel, draw the young men of Harlem into the avenues of the Upper East Side. Their dream is *Vogue*; the object of their desire is the Other exhibited therein – another skin color, another class, above all another sex: at last, to be something, i.e. to be something different from what they are themselves. To this end, there is the 'Ball,' the exclusive object of the film; with a passion the documentation immortalizes the ball, just as the ball immortalizes the image of fashion, restoring to it the passion that it had long lost.

These boys, these men, live in order to costume themselves for the ball, to get up on the stage that is their life – in a style of movement which owes its name and not a few of its poses to the dream stage of all dream stages and which must naturally be called 'vogueing.' Most of all, they like to dress as women. Shakespeare's Drag Queen (from *As You Like It*) is the tried and tested theatrical model: the man as woman. They parade down the catwalk as hip-swinging models in designer fashion, as Las Vegas showgirls with feathers bobbing and sequins flashing, as all-American stars tossing blonde curls, as girls from the corner with the gum-chewing sexiness of teenagers. A few want not merely to dress as women, but to be women. They take their desire for the other (a desire for non-identity) with a desire for this identity. So they wish for a sex change – as if then reality could begin, as if one could become a woman. Others know that it is not identity that they desire, but rather the play with identity: 'I am not a woman, I emulate women,' says Pepper Labeija, *mother* of the Labeija house. But, as Plato was aware, nothing is less innocent, more dangerous than mimesis: Identity, Being itself, is unmasked as an 'as if,' as a game. Playing woman leads directly into the caricatural exaggeration of the role. Medical naturalization takes the sting from the process of denaturalization that this play sets in motion. What the drag queen brings to light and on to the catwalk is 'woman' as disguise.

The *mise en scène* of the genuine lets the genuine appear as *mise en scène*. The world which is here imitated is the world of the television, of the models, of the fashion magazine. It is the world of appearance, which produces the effect of the real, the real as effect. What makes the ball into the most important thing in the world, what lets Paris burn, is the desire to appear on the stage, to stand in the realm of appearance, to be a star, a model. There is something fascinating about the production of appearance, about the staging of the real as appearance. In the process, we see reality as something which is being pursued by all, and, at the same time, we see why it is that *all* have to pursue it. In the dizzying insight into the reality-effect created by the system of simulacra, the excluded (blacks, gays) triumph over the impenetrable and blind power whose emblem, the Empire State Building, stands like a fortress across the East River. The ideal woman today is the transvestite: the staged mimesis of the ball of Harlem brings it to light. Transvestites are not only popular models, they are also ideal customers. They have arrived then: Livingston's film is the funeral hymn not only of the victims of the epidemic, remembered in the credits, but also of the ball and of vogueing. The latter, like the break-dance before it, declines into a tourist attraction, and, with Madonna's video of the same name, vogueing is definitively incorporated into the mainstream. In the film, the paradox of the simulacra is doubled one more time, for the last time. Only in the exposed mimesis of the appearance does 'the real thing' come into being: two years later it becomes usable for *Vogue*, though, as the film shows, thereby loses its realness. In the end, Paris burns.

At the end of *Paris is Burning*, the authentic no longer stands in the sign of reliable reference, not even in that of the death of the actors, the long lists of whom keep the audience in the seats and the aisles for long minutes. Not, in any case, in the sign of genuine gold on whose standard the adjacent metropolis is built; rather, in the sign of the sign itself: of the drop earrings brought back from a tour of Japan by a successful ball-king, for example, in whose false gold (studded with illegible signs) the logo of 'Gaultier' is resplendent.

Fashion is disguise, a disguise which operates not according to fancy, but following a determinate code. The code pretends merely to represent reality; one clothes oneself 'appropriately' when one dresses oneself as a man or woman, and as representative of a particular civil profession, according to one's gender and social position. Here, fashion disguises the fact that it disguises. The message runs something like: I appear as what I am: I am identical with myself, I am authentic; I do not cheat, do not deceive, do not counterfeit. This naturalization of the code not only does not correspond to reality, it does not correspond to its own reality – which is that of a rhetorical effect. Authenticity is an effect, one among others that fashion can produce. Postfashion exhibits this effect for what it is; as an effect. In this sense, it is an anti-authentic discourse.

Jean-Paul Gaultier's response to the perfect woman, sold with particular perfection by Frederick's of Hollywood, is a good

example. Frederick's of Hollywood dominates the market with
a catalogue which banishes fashion, by revealing the point at
which the secret wishes and declared aims of the customers are
compatible. After the Second World War, its founder missed the
satin and lace nightshirts 'that went with every mental picture
I'd had of girls, who did turn me on when I was in the army'[13]
– and he knew how to remedy the fact. He had also learnt that
not all women had the form of his dreams. He set to work, to
make sure that women could be women (just as men could be
successful soldiers). The slogan of the women's movement for
equal opportunity could be changed into equal opportunity in
the eyes of men. Women are not like men; they are *for* men. 'I
wanted to make ANY woman her most feminine, alluring, sexy
self. I knew that there had to be ways to reproportion women
and give every lovable one of them EQUAL OPPORTUNITY
in the eyes of men!'[14] So he drew in the waist, padded and lifted
legs, bottom and breasts – and made it not only look but even
feel genuine. What, for Frederick, was natural and therefore
had to be hidden, for Gaultier has to be exhibited as artificial
process. He sells as a pin-up a dress cut and padded after the
measures of the ideal woman, in which the breast and bottom
padding, the waste and thigh cut are turned outward, in order
that the whole process becomes visible. From the fetish 'woman'
emerges the mask 'woman.' It is not only those who, as in *Paris
is Burning*, are not biological women or those who, like the
customers of Frederick's, have to adjust themselves to the correct
standards, who have to produce themselves as women. The days
of biologically perfect women can also be entirely taken up
with this undertaking. At work in the industry responsible for
the creation of the fetish of the feminine – as saleswomen in
luxurious stores, as models – the women acquire the reflection
of this fetish – and thereby make their 'career'; i.e. they catch
the man. They, no less than the wealthy woman, can acquire
the bewitching aura of femininity. Class differences retreat in
favor of the signifier 'femininity.' The object of feminine desire
is unclear – is it the man or is it fashion? Whose object of desire
is the woman under these conditions? That of the man or that
of the woman?

In the nineteenth and twentieth centuries the desire for fashion
becomes the feminine passion *par excellence*: everything is
sacrificed to it. The will to be *à la mode* is stronger than the will

to be loved, so strong that even financial ruin is not too high a price to pay. It does not only lead off the path of virtue: often enough it leads straight into death. What brings women into temptation is not the man – who is rather a means to an end – but the craving for clothing. In Zola's *Paradise of Women* the women stagger with feverishly burning eyes, dazed to the point of exhaustion with the shopping fever, through fantastically draped mountains of cloth, through splendidly coloured gleaming silks, through snowy delights of lace; in the spell of this fascination, trembling with excitement, they ruin themselves and their families, throw fortunes out the window, gamble away class and position, descend from nobility to theft. Henry James' Mlle Noémie, seeing two very elegantly clothed women in the Louvre, has the feeling 'that the happiness of having such a train would be worth any price,' and quickly resolves to become a coquette.[15] Madame Bovary's ruin, one may recall, is fatally accelerated by her taste for clothing and finery, and Edith Wharton's Lily, in *The House of Mirth*, accepts money from married men for such things, but then does not want to pay the price, falls nonetheless in a murky light, and in the end takes her own life. And who has not had a girlfriend whose depression was conjured away at no other price than through an excursion into the glittering and beguiling world of fashion?

The fashion world is a world in which female desire, as desire of and for the other comes to light. Masks of femininity are sketched out and tried on; preparations are made for the daily performance. Feminine no less than masculine desire is directed at the 'woman' as the epitome of desireability and therefore it is a matter of producing this 'femininity.' For, as is well-known, women are not born, but become 'women,' make themselves into 'women.' Fashion itself can take up various possible stances towards this state of affairs. It can play it down, minimalize it. The naturalization of the 'woman' is the dominant tendency of the bourgeois understanding of fashion, which, however, is always again provoked and successfully subverted by the *demi-monde*. The *demi-monde* is like the child in the fable of the emperor's new clothes, who speaks out what the grown-up world of bourgeois interests leaves unspoken. Certainly, there is a bourgeois version of the fable, in which decent dress affirms itself against the unjustified, vain authority of the Ancien Régime as the most natural thing in the world; but the dictum 'clothes make the man' is always latent in the moral of the story. As moving force of fashion, the *demi-monde* reveals the purpose of dress and costume. Not that this excludes the reciprocal desire, within the *demi-monde*, to be a completely 'normal woman.' The 'decent' woman's ability to be inconspicuously elegant and stylish, discreetly made-up and restrained in the exhibition of femininity – all this is merely an acceptable face of the same fashion that is represented by the *demi-monde*. In order that the effect is natural, all traces of artificiality and masquerade have to be carefully erased. True fashion, for Jil Sander, underlines the true self of the woman. She does not conform to any external dictate, does not invent herself: she finds what suits her – that is, her true self. She expresses her originality, in just the same way as thousands of other women: with Jil Sander. The tasteful self-fashioning, which Jil Sanders markets in expensively inconspicuous form, is the final and perfect counterpart to post-modern fashion. Irony, parody and hyperbole and other reflexive figures bring distance into the passion for fashion, and show that which made the *demi-monde* scandalous, if in moderated form: woman as culture, not nature.

Rousseau, apostle of nature, father of the bourgeois republic and founder of its gender politics was altogether conscious of the rhetorical character of the 'natural feminine.' With far-reaching consequences, not only for fashion, but also for that which is to be expressed through fashion, he decided on the particular mode of staging femininity, with which we are still today contending. It is not irrelevant then to recall, if only in outline, Rousseau's influential scenario: here we find the stage directions for the primarily French *mode de cent ans*, and, by the same token, the decisive counter-indications for the forms of postfashion. In *Emile*, Rousseau's *Bildungsroman*, the whole fate of the little girl is already decided with the pleasure she takes in her doll. She will herself become a doll, as girl and as woman:

> Observe a little girl spending the day around her doll, constantly changing its clothes, dressing and undressing it hundreds and hundreds of times, continuously seeking new combinations of ornaments – well or ill-matched, it makes no difference. Her fingers lack adroitness, her taste is not yet formed, but already the inclination reveals itself. In this eternal occupation time flows without her thinking

of it. She even forgets meals. She is hungrier for adornment than for food. But, you will say, she adorns her doll and not her person. Doubtless. She sees her doll and does not see herself. She can do nothing for herself… She is entirely in her doll and she puts all her coquetry into it. She will not always leave it there. She awaits the moment when she will be her own doll.[16]

This perception is in the background of Rousseau's doctrine of authenticity: Rousseau establishes a rhetoric of anti-fashion – of the authentic – that will itself soon become fashionable. Postfashion owes much to the reversal of this Rousseauian manoeuvre. For Rousseau, the art of fashion should consist in underlining natural beauty, as a supplement to natural, given beauty. The effect is to be centered on the person, not on his or her clothing. With this, the whole bourgeois rhetoric of inconspicuousness, of the style that is not one, sets in. The determination of the concept of woman that is part of this staging of the natural is of great significance for the bourgeois image of woman. The woman is determined by the norms of modesty, of *pudeur*, terms which stand in for a definite relation of the female self to herself: fashion is the perceived danger against which this model is worked out: postfashion is its reversal.

The adult woman has to learn to forget this ability to see herself as her own doll, the ability to see herself with the eyes of another, that is, she has to interiorize it, make it unconscious, and therefore innocent. In this innocence lies her femininity. Women have to dress as 'women,' and more than this, they have to act as if they were not able to reflect on this process, in order to guarantee its efficacy.

The antithesis to the ideal here constructed is the women of Paris. Rousseau does not hesitate to grant them the title of best-dressed women in the world – albeit with the qualification that it is they who stand in greatest need of this skill. In contrast to provincial women, the Parisians dominate fashion and are not themselves dominated by it. They introduce fashion in order to make up for their natural faults, which – still according to Rousseau – are greater than those of women from elsewhere. The end result is that they are actually no longer women. Instead of modestly blushing under the gaze of men, they shamelessly and directly return the gaze of the man, and it is the men who end up lowering their eyes in confusion. Ever conscious of their own appearance in the eyes of others, they have reached the point of testing their own effect in the eyes of men, which, for a woman – in Rousseau's eyes – is inevitably to deprive oneself of all effect.

For Rousseau, it is the women of the aristocracy who are least of all women, precisely because it is they who most ostentatiously display their feminine allures. The masquerade that is femininity appears behind the mask. Aristocratic women wear a lot of rouge, low-cut *décolletés*, ornament their cleavage: they are so shameless that they cannot even be described to the modest Julie. In short, the women of the French aristocracy makes themselves look like whores, because that is the only way to prevent themselves being imitated by the bourgeois. 'Ceasing to be women, for fear of being confused with other women, they choose their rank over their sex, and imitate the women of pleasure, in order that they will not be imitated.'[17]

In the wake of the Parisian aristocracy, the *demi-monde* of the nineteenth century disavows the ideal of femininity prescribed by Rousseau to the citizens of the Republic. Most congenial to the male citizens, as we have observed, was that their wives should not merely live up to the prescribed image of 'woman,' that they should not merely produce this ideal, but that they should dissimulate the process of production. All biologically female beings should appear with complete naturalness as 'women.' By becoming all too expert in this process, the Parisian woman endangered the progress of the Revolution. Fashion is their secret, a secret which has preserved its explosive power, and which always again unmasks Rousseau's 'nature of woman' as wishful thinking. Within the history of fashion, the history of this secret knowledge can perhaps best be told as a history of cross-dressings, as a game of hide and seek with gender, in which woman appears as 'woman,' 'woman' appears as dandy, man as 'woman,' woman as man as 'woman,' and unisex as superman.

When the fashion of the moderns, as a travesty of genders, exhibits 'le sexe' and virtualizes it in a play of signifiers, then this demystification, as the demystification of a fiction, has nothing to do with the temptations of the flesh, which in the Protestant ethics of Rousseau functioned very conveniently as a kind of premium of temptation, lending the authority of tradition to his own constructions. Rousseau's rhetorical ruse, considering woman as nature and pinning her to this determination, draws on the older myth of the original sin and the guilt of Eve. But the shamelessness of the *demi-monde* is not a product of fallen creatureliness, no more than is the regained innocence in Rousseau. The opposition of 'clothed' and 'naked,' veiled and stripped, is therefore entirely inappropriate to the characterization of fashion. To hold to these criteria is, so to speak, one of the 'puritan pleasures,' on which the success of Rousseau's design has rested up until the present day. One holds to decency (at least superficially), not out of a genuine concern with decency, but because of gender politics. The fashion of the last thirty years has here made a considerable contribution.

In the meantime, it is clear to almost everyone that the naked breasts of models have basically nothing in common with the naked breasts of Playgirls, the very incarnation of *Puritan Pleasures*. Precisely the progressive baring of the female body in fashion has shown the absurdity of equating the two. What is exposed – and disguised – with fashion is not, in the first place, the attractions of the body, but rather the erotics of intelligence, a play of *Geist und Kleid*. To learn fashion as this subtle play is equivalent to learning the art of reading literature, an art which, as Baudelaire and Mallarmé openly avowed, had brought them to the best part of their understanding and their production. The topos of this 'knowledge' is the difference which is known as 'femininity.'

Notes

1. Charles Baudelaire 'A une passante' and 'A une mendiante rousse,' from 'Les tableaux parisiennes,' in *Les Fleurs du Mal*, ed. A. Adam, Paris, 1961.
2. Walter Benjamin *The Arcades Project*, trans. Howard Eiland and Kevin McLaughlin, Cambridge 1999, Folios 3, 2.
3. Paul Morand, *L'allure de Chanel*, Paris 1976, p. 140
4. Walter Benjamin 'On some motifs in Baudelaire,' in *Illuminations*, New York 1969, ed. and with an introduction by Hannah Arendt, trans. Harry Zohn, pp. 155–201.

5. Translation follows Benjamin 'On some motifs in Baudelaire,' p. 169.
6. Heinrich Heine, 'Die Reise nach Genua,' in *Reisebilder*, Chap. 17. *Sämtliche Schriften III*, Munich, 1969, p. 349.
7. Benjamin, *The Arcades Project*, p. 79 (translation modified).
8. Benjamin, *Illuminations*, p. 169.
9. Benjamin 'On some motifs in Baudelaire,' p. 163.
10. Anselm Haverkamp, 'Dialektisches Bild,' in *Figura cryptica. Theorie der literarichen Latenz*, Frankfurt, 2002, p. 56ff.
11. William Faulkner, *Mosquitoes*, New York 1955 (1923), p. 23.
12. Georges Brassens' 'Les sabots d'Hélène,' in *Georges Brassens par excellence IV* (Philips C-72-CX-253).
13. Laura and Janusz Gottwald, *Frederick's of Hollywood 1947–73 – 26 Years of Mail Order Seduction*, New York 1970 (1867), p. 9.
14. Frederick's of Hollywood catalogue, 1955, p. 37
15. Henry James' *The American*, New York 1981 (1867), p. 195.
16. Jean-Jacques Rousseau, *Emile or On Education*, ed. Allan Bloom, New York 1979, Book V, Part III, p. 367.
17. Jean-Jacques Rousseau, *La Nouvelle Héloïse* in *Œuvres complètes*, Vol. II, eds Bernard Gagnebin and Marcel Raymond, Paris 1964, p. 268.

3

High and Low: The End of a Century of Fashion

In 1967, at the height of structuralism, Roland Barthes ascribed the prestige of fashion to its link to the aristocracy.[1] The association is in fact altogether conventional. Barthes was referring, of course, to the French aristocracy. This did not need spelling out since, at the end of the 1960s, fashion was still self-evidently French, and the aristocracy in this context could only be the French aristocracy. French supremacy in questions of taste had been uncontested since the seventeenth century, and fashion could only be international inasmuch as it cited or invoked French fashion. One of the first cultural exports which liberated France sent into the USA in 1947 consisted in a *Théâtre de la Mode*, a construction in which, because of shortages of cloth, miniature wire mannequins modeled miniature creations by designers such as Schiaparelli, Balenciaga, Patou, Pierre Balmain, Jacques Fath, Hermès, or Nina Ricci, in settings such as the opera, the ball, the park, or at a picnic.[2] With these little dolls, the *couturiers* were carrying on a tradition which had already served to promote Paris fashion throughout the world in Napoleon's time. The dolls were banned by Napoleon, however, even before they could be replaced by fashion magazines, because they could be used to transport secret messages. This link between fashion and foreign politics surfaced again when Napoleon prohibited the importation of cloth from England, and obliged the ladies of the land to limit themselves to articles of national origin.

Already in the time of Henry James, one could speak of 'pretty looking girls in Parisian dresses' in New York, and still today Paris fashion capitalizes on the aura it has created for itself.[3] The split between 'the Emperor' Lagerfeld and Ines de la Fressange, the exclusive model in the House of Chanel, gave an indication of the peculiar complexity of the interests invested in this export. In 1989, the 200th anniversary of the French Revolution, Ms. de la Fressange appeared patriotically wrapped in the tricolor as an allegory of liberty. For Karl Lagerfeld this was not compatible with the image of international elegance. Perhaps it had occurred to him that it was the Revolution which had broken the international standard of the aristocracy, and marked the beginning of the decline into bourgeois order and nationalism.

For Parisian fashion is essentially linked to aristocratic society, to its conspicuous consumption, to excess and the unconditional passion for elegance. Devastating *chic*, frivolous luxury, capriciousness and arbitrariness are part and parcel of the ideal of stylistic perfection, and only serve to heighten the inimitable attraction of the fashion world. Fashion asserts its own will, in apparent independence of the law of the market; it tyrannizes over the passage of time and bends the rationality of economics to the rhythm of the seasons. In this sense, it has remained sovereign and aristocratic. As *haute couture*, fashion was the fashion of the select few who were willing and able to pay to hold on to the dreams of a better time. Fashion represented another, less prosaic world, in which aristocratic displays of splendor were still possible. The creators of these fashions sought fashion in the exotic, far from everyday vulgarity, in distant lands, in art, in the museum. Christian Dior withdrew into nature, hoping to capture the light on a stone, the swinging of a tree. Hubert de Givenchy created clothes which evoke the joys of elegant country life. This fashion was opposed to the street: it attracted not the most beautiful women, but the rich and famous. The *spiritus loci* of solemn elegance had become all-pervasive. Yves Saint

Laurent, the first, in his 1960 winter collection, to introduce street fashion such as leather jackets and turtleneck pullovers into *haute couture*, clearly came to believe that the street could be tamed to the purposes of *haute couture*. In 1978, when he again took over some details from street fashion – pointed collars, small hats, shoes with tassels – it was in order to bring a little bit of wit into *haute couture* – the 'freedom of the street, the arrogance and provocation of the punks, for example,' in his words – but 'all of this naturally with dignity, luxury, style.'[4] Exactly this, however, 'dignity, luxury, and style,' was what had definitively driven the street out of fashion.

As has been underscored by a long series of more or less problematic jokes and caricatures, a significant part of the clientèle of the *haute couture* now belongs not to the European 'top ten thousand' but to regimes of dubious standing in the Third World. Thickly veiled Saudi princesses believe themselves to be participating in a world which no longer exists. Jean-Paul Gaultier in his photo-novel *A nous deux, la mode* parodied the late colonialism effect in several such regimes, mostly complicit with American imperialism.[5] The hero, who is French, is sent to Manila where he represents Cardin, and exploits the appeal of Paris to such good effect that he is even able to sell his customers an apron with flowers on it as the height of elegance. The decline of the pretentions of fashion is registered by Gaultier, who highlights his own petit bourgeois origin by adopting the petit bourgeois and slightly outdated genre of the photo-novel. But postfashion is more than merely an anti-fashion: the rebellion against fashion is just the starting point of something different.

The century of fashion is over: the very idea of Paris fashion is at an end – even an anti-fashion could not save it. The reasons for this cannot be adequately grasped within the terms of the self-understanding of the old fashion or the sociology of fashion. The new situation is expressed in the reversal of the relationship between fashion-creator and imitator. Since the 1970s, it has no longer been the case that fashions are launched by the aristocracy or the bourgeoisie, and then filter down into the general population: fashion now moves 'upwards,' from the street into the salons of *haute couture* where it is adapted and imitated. On the one hand, the fashion-buying public has increased; on the other hand, this public no longer determines trends, but reacts to trends that emerge from subcultures.

What from a sociological point of view would appear as a change of direction in fact reflects a new concept of fashion, one which resolutely uses non-fashionable elements to create the avant-garde effect of a fashion beyond fashion. The designers of the 1980s seal the end of the era of fashion-creators, and, with some self-irony, favor trends which lie outside the obsolete perception of the fashionable. They destroy the ideas on which the Western Paris-based fashion system is based. The Far-Eastern 'aesthetic of poverty' counters old-European-aristocratic conceptions of the 'aestheticization of the everyday.' Certainly, Japanese fashion communicates with Western anti-fashion over a cultural abyss, and one must here be aware of the distorting effects of translation. But one thing at least becomes clear with the bridge that has been created: fashion will no longer strictly divide, whether classes, age groups, or genders. Nothing could be more out of date than to clothe oneself as 'woman,' as 'man' or as 'lady.'

In the West, fashion becomes 'carnivalistic': it cancels the divisions of classes and genders, and, more than this, it exposes the function of costume and disguise at work in categories of class and gender. This second step is decisive. For the cancellation of the divisions of gender and class has to remain virtual, a gesture of protest; its exposure as disguise on the other hand, tells the truth – somewhat as it was told in the fable of the Emperor's new clothes, well before the era of modern fashion. The earlier aesthetic avant-garde had already undertaken to dissolve the schema of gender, age and class as merely relational qualities, and, at the same time, to destroy the idea of fashion as aristocratic, luxurious, elegant and beautiful. Accordingly, the avant-garde in fashion is anti-idealistic and non-conformist: it is experimental and aims to shock, rather than to create beauty and perfection. It works with discontinuities and stark contrasts rather than with the harmony of lines. In its style the new fashion avant-garde draws on the strategies of the old avant-garde, especially when it is a matter of attacking the classical *haute couture*. This may be why Yves Saint Laurent, on whom women as diverse as Marguerite Yourcenar and Marguerite Duras swore, scarcely twenty years later gives the impression of a kind of design well-suited to the shopkeeper from the corner. In any case, the avant-garde beginnings of a postfashion have been successful in one point. Even after Fashion, style is not a matter of the practical, the good, the comfortable, or the natural. Postfashion opposes itself to quiet elegance, but also to comfortable sportiness, to Benetton, Esprit and Gap no less than to Hermès silk, pearl chain, cashmere twinset, and Brooks Brothers. With the growing readiness for ugliness, for the grotesque and the ridiculous, with the citations of a 'perverse' sexuality, postfashion exceeds its avant-garde beginnings; it becomes self-distanced, self-ironic, even if, in its weaker moments, it falls back on a tendency to *épater le bourgeois*. The punk, like his prototype the dandy, cannot altogether free himself from his origin; the one from the high, the other from the low end of the social spectrum, both are faithful to a milieu that they transform, but from which they also draw the force of their gesture.

The punks decisively shattered the established ideals of beauty and decency for a whole fashion generation. Clothed in all black, they generally wanted to appear as anti-fashionable. But they were also the first to create their clothing from the cast-offs and refuse materials of the city: the shiny plastic of garbage bags, the remains of old tires, from rubber and tin. Punk fashion actively positioned itself under the sign of the artificiality of both sexes. Men and women colored their hair pink, green or blue, and put it up into fantastic towering structures which in their splendor recalled the outlandish head-wear of Marie Antoinette. The punk body occupied a position exterior to that which is marketed as natural and healthy; punks introduced 'barbaric' practices such as the piercing of ears, noses and lips. Their clothes were torn, worn, and dirty, and aggressively underlined poverty: instead of a lapdog they carried a rat: the mixture of cuteness and repulsiveness, the pathetic appearance of the naked tails created an ingeniously ambivalent effect. Both sexes devoted all their time to self-styling, an indulgence which in the bourgeois society of the post-war period was at best allowed to women. Styling here does not erase itself in the interest of a final effect of naturalness: it is exposed in its artificiality. The young un-employed of the big cities refused the credo of a society for which the essence of man was entirely identified with work and career. Comme des Garçons recognized punk as a revolutionary intervention in the idea of fashion, and offered a homage to it in its winter collection of 1991. Punk was too uncompromising to establish itself as a lasting stylistic possibility, but its sting remained even in the diluted, popularized offenses against the canons of good taste on the part of popular culture.

Postfashion is very much dependent on populist myths and their motives, on the jackets of Hell's Angels, the caps of basketball teams, the hotpants of motorcycle girls. What would be left of the winter collection of 1991 of Yamamoto and Gaultier without the drag queen and the sugar daddy? What would be left of Chanel without biker jackets, and faded jeans? In the collections of the last years there has been hardly one which has not featured sneakers. The latest development is the cooperation between Adidas and Yamamoto. What would the fashion of the 1990s have been without the cheap kitsch and trash fashion of the street? Even the vogue for wearing underwear as 'over-wear,' popular for years now, comes from the street. With this last trend, the masquerade becomes to the highest extent possible a thematization of disguise itself. What was supposed to remain concealed and give figure to the body – the girdle, the bra – is now openly exhibited. The whole apparatus of hiding and revealing, of the forbidden, secret gaze solicited by pin-up girls – the garter, the bra, the corsage as tantalizing signs of sexuality – is openly displayed in its costume-function as illusion-generating: here fashion offers a look behind the scenes at the mechanics of lust, and appropriates the fashion of lust in the cause of the lust for fashion. This fashion has an obscene effect, precisely because it is not obscene. From this exhibition of desire, Dolce & Gabbana are able to generate the capital of a doubled eroticism. They bring onto the public stage of the street what was once reserved for the private pleasure of the ever-same individual universal – namely the costuming of the women for the purpose of pornography.

The revival of the fashion of the 1970s, with its euphoria for synthetic materials, which have since become irreversibly associated with cheapness – shiny nylon and acrylic – bell-bottoms and unbuttoned shirts, tight pullovers, and gaudy colors, does not intend a nostalgic return to a better past. It rediscovers a fashion which in all its ridiculousness, and precisely because it is from yesterday, is again from today. It is not the fashion of our grandmothers or of our fathers. It is our own, that which we ourselves wore twenty-five years earlier. It has the uncanniness of that which is only too familiar. What is rediscovered is not its beauty, but its outrageousness. Through this play with the times, postfashion becomes harder, seeking stylistic satisfaction in the shock of ugliness.

Another trend is the deliberate stylelessness that pretends complete indifference to received conventions of style. In opposition to the principle of combination represented by the suit, one cultivates indifference in questions of 'good taste' and 'appropriateness,' and arbitrariness and clash in color, cut and material. The random foray into the closet, the mood of the moment, manifests itself in the form of an arbitrary aggregate. One is certainly not naked, but by no means 'dressed.' Tulle and tweed, velvet and plastic, cashmere and nylon, parka and lace dress, denim jacket and dress skirt, lurex pullover and flannel pants, all are mixed: carelessness is artfully simulated; items which clearly do not go together are worn the one on top of the other and compelled to a comical coexistence. The code of relations governing the association of certain cuts and certain materials is played with and transgressed. This principle of the apparent indeterminate negation, which had been virtuosically exploited by Gaultier, later found its way into the pseudo-*haute couture*, where it was tamed and naturalized by Lacroix.

Along with the reversal of high and low, the carnevalization of relations, and the populist dissolution of the borders that mark out stylistic regions, postfashion is characterized by a decisive change in the relation of fashion to time. The *mode de cent ans* is always oriented towards a triumph over time, in the last instance towards a triumph over death. By the brilliance of the moment, fashion blinds to the work of time. Aging comes to be associated with the category of the *démodé*, the opposite of fashion. The fleeting existence and rapid transformation of fashions reflect the pressure of time, which ever again has to be trumped with the new and the newest.

Hence the tendency of the *mode de cent ans* to flee the everyday world into idylls, in which time stands still, or to displace itself into other times and other structures of time, into a time outside time. It delights in the evocation of the kind of distant exotic fairytale lands that provided the setting to innumerable erotic fantasies for the orientalism of the nineteenth century. Freed from the restrictions of real sexuality, one loses oneself in the beguiling fantasies of slave and tyrant, of which there is already a foretaste in Delacroix, and which feature prominently in Proust's *Recherche*: the *Thousand and One Nights* fashion of Poiret, the splendor of the Chinese court in Saint Laurent take one into such worlds of erotic exoticism. The attraction of creations such as Paco Rabanne's space clothing or Montana and Mugler's superwomen in shining metal science-fiction costumes with their euphoric relation to technology and their Amazon appeal is likewise not least due to their extra-temporal situation. The endless fascination for ethno-fashion, which lends the requisite hippy chic to labels such as Voyage, could also be discussed in this context.

This fashion reanimates the art and the styles of the ancient Egyptians, the Renaissance, the eighteenth century, Victorianism; classicism, in particular, is reinvented with ever-renewed enthusiasm. 'Modern' borrowings are also entirely possible, as is shown by the fashion for triangular headscarves with folk patterns based on Russian realism, a nostalgic tribute to socialism after its fall. In fashion, post-modernism is not a new manner of transforming the past: it has often remained rather a variation of historicism, a historicism which is as old as fashion itself, even if it may have appeared for the brief moment of modernity that there could be a direct development to the 'silhouette of the modern.'[6] Certainly, this historicism is capable of a hybrid fusing of styles that goes beyond mere historical preservation and reproduction. Its strength, however, lies in forgetting: it is above all not an art of memory. On the contrary: fashion is one of the most effective filtering mechanisms of forgetting, a method of effacing the past through its reanimation. The longing for a place beyond history corresponds to the longing for an eternal present. On the occasion of a collection of Yves Saint Laurent, the American *Vogue* wrote in 1976: 'Here we can see how artful fashion has become in its interpretation of history. It is not a nostalgia for the past, but for the eternal present, beyond the past.'[7] In the reactivation of what once was, mortality as such is extinguished. By the same token, however, the history of fashion now becomes the clearest manifestation of its own mortality, the most reliable medium for preserving the destructive traces of time that it represses at the moment of its initial appearance.

Things are different in postfashion: it seeks to draw time, and makes itself into a new 'art of memory.' The signs and traces of time are the stuff from which this fashion is made, replacing the traditional material of fashion, 'the stuff of which dreams are made.' In the extreme case, clothing becomes a sign of mortality, an index of time that has passed. Already made out of worn materials, it does not remind one of another time, but rather shows a trace of memory, in which duration is discontinuously inscribed. The duration of its own production, the amount of work-time that has gone into it, is exactly readable in the finished product. Often it bears witness, as in time-lapse photography, to the historical development of certain styles. If the defining structure of *la mode de cent ans* consisted in the cyclical revival of forgotten fashions, postfashion tends to make time as duration into its material. In order to take the conspicuous sheen of newness from his clothes, Yamamoto has, since the early 1970s, pre-washed most of the clothes he sells. Comme des Garçons works handmade embroidered materials, from the Near East for example, into its clothes. Its own materials are not smoothly weaved, but contain irregularities, 'flaws.' And their lace sweater, in the judgment of the unfailingly charming press, looked like it had only just survived a moth attack in a homeless person's bag. Romeo Gigli uses silks which shine with the faded luster of past splendor: he learnt the technique for the production of these materials in countries barely touched by the Industrial Revolution. With a dash of sadomasochism, Dolce & Gabbana sell men's jackets in which the shocks of a harsh urban life are already imprinted: they are decorated with cigarette burns, rips. Margiela creates skirts out of flea-market scarves. It is not a matter here of ecological recycling, of the creation of the new out of the old for pragmatic-ethical reasons. On the contrary, it is a matter of showing the old as old – an altogether aesthetic maneuver.

Here again the precursors are the dandies who had their clothes pre-worn, or slept on them, so that they looked crumpled and worn. The hectic pace of fashion was countered with the composure proper to aristocracy. Coco Chanel reported that the Earl of Winchester, the richest man in the world, never gave the impression of wearing new clothes. The effect is now a mass phenomenon. The increasing success of second-hand clothes and thrift shops belongs to this trend. It has very little to do with frugality. In flea markets, buyers seek out clothes that are not only not new, but that emphatically belong to other periods. Along with the clothes, one wears also the spirits of the past. This confirms that fashion – contrary to its reputation – has become an art of memory.

It is up to date to be resolutely no longer up to date. Rather, the fashion is to wear 'time' – not the hectic time of the latest fashion, or the nostalgic time of the past, but rather a forgotten, other time. Fashion (after Fashion) has become the site at which the repressed other surfaces. The saved other can often be then

discovered as a repressed other self: handicraft, threatened by
unified global culture, is saved in that which is about to extin-
guish it. Into the world of jeans, sneakers, and business suits, the
triumph of Western clothing, fashion inscribes traces of another
time, in which another duration is visible; auratic moments beyond
the habitualized, vulgarized shocks: but also sober moderation
in the nonchalance of irregular materials, the charm of what is
incomplete, individual. In the end, the border between kitsch,
camp and art can be difficult to make out in this encounter of the
familiar and the foreign. Nothing therefore can outdo the intact
otherness of foreign cultures, the abssyal distance preserved even
in the movement of approach.

Japanese fashion exposed the false conventionality of Western
fashion. And worldly Paris fashion had little with which to
counter a foreign form-consciousness that failed to be seduced by
it. Gaultier alone was able to respond, in mobilizing the resources
of popular culture. The provocation of the Japanese clearly
signified a very exactly measured negation: the new fashion,
originating from a land whose upper levels were firmly under
the influence of French fashion, knew what it was up against. A
unanimous cry of protest went through the French press as Rei
Kawakubo gave her first Paris show with Comme des Garçons in
1981. For Comme des Garçons was not attacking any particular
fashion-creator, but rather the defining idea of fashion itself.
Kawakubo's collection rejected the idea of the beautiful, the
noble, the perfect; it erased the difference of the sexes and sought
to define a relation of body and clothing that was no longer
based in hiding, revealing and exhibiting. The provocation of
the French name of the label pointed to the fact that the dignity
and ceremoniousness of the Parisian fashion world is here an
object of wit and parody. Kawakubo's clothes were no longer
cut to the body, no longer sat as if they had been poured on
– the most important criterion of *haute couture*. On the contrary,
these clothes could be altered by the wearer, turned inside out, a
jacket could become a pullover, a skirt could become a dress.

In Japanese fashion, the idea of the dress as second skin,
the relation of dress and body, is conceptualized in a radically
different manner, and subjected to experimental modifications.
Sometimes, the body is wrapped up and tied like a package.
In Yamamoto, the shape of the body is completely estranged
by three-dimensional sculptures, alluding to the paper folds of

origami. In Miyake, the movement of the body, transmitted to the clothing through fine foldings, is transformed into an unexpected event. The result is surprising indeed: the dress, and with it the body, forms itself into another sculpture with every breath. The flow of movement is arrested as a film in slow motion is cut into single images.[8] The predominance of black in Comme des Garçons underlined such effects. Dresses needed only three sizes; they could be folded together at will. They were asymmetrical; the seam on one side was longer than on the other; they had holes. At first sight, the wearer appeared terribly poor. On a second look, one might think of the Earl of Winchester. For the new ideal is not clothes in which one makes an appearance, but clothes in which one lives and works. Clothes become a part of the self, grow to be part of the body, wear out on it. The theatrical element of luxury and expenditure is foreign to this approach. To counter this Gaultier summons up the whole extravagant masquerade of the native theatrical resources. Between these two possibilities – the forgotten riches of popular culture and the foreign form ideal – the one neo-Romantic, the other a kind of remote classicism, fashion plays itself out at the end of the century.

Wim Wenders on Yamamoto, Gaultier on Gaultier

Wim Wenders' film of 1990, *On Cities and Clothes*, was the result of a commission from the Centre George Pompidou for a film about fashion. It presents itself as a reflection on the loss of the original with the power of reproduceability, the impossibility of distinguishing between original and copy, the replacement of media such as photography and film by digital media such as the video camera. One sometimes has the impression of a director who has picked up some very interesting ideas, at a party perhaps, about Benjamin, Baudrillard and Kittler, and would now like to give a report on them. The basic intention of the film, so steeped in post-modern reflections, is to present a comparison of media: the high-technology digital camera learns in the romantic medium of Far-Eastern clothing to discover and reflect on the authentic life betrayed by Western clothing. Wenders confronts fashion, in its bad Western development (here the familiar denunciations of fashion are implicitly presupposed), with the simple, happy life offered by Japanese *savoir vivre*.

His hero, Yamamoto, who cooperates in an engagingly non-committal way, is presented as irreplaceable *créateur* who can teach fashion how once again to become authentic. Wenders has experienced and worn this uniqueness on his own body. It is transmitted from the hand of the master, who cuts out himself each of the pieces that he designs. One sees here the return of the aesthetics of genius which had passed into *haute couture*. Yamamoto hand signs, with the authority of his authorship, for the authenticity of each of his creations. His *griffe*, the signature of his productions, is not printed, but signed by hand. It maintains a 'motivated,' iconic, non-arbitrary relation to the master's creations. In a period saturated with the jargon of structuralism, the metaphor of language naturally does not fail to appear. The fashion-creator Yamamoto discovers his own inimitable language. Certainly, the thrust of structuralism is missed in the emphatic Romantic identification. For signification originates – if one takes Saussure's teaching seriously – not through identity but through difference. Here one sees what remains unexpressed in the conciliatory attitude of Yamamoto. For what Wenders' film presents Yamamoto as attaining remains in his clothing definitely out of reach, and precisely in this lies their unique character. It is no surprise then that clothes appear in the film only in passing, and the refinement of particular pieces is not thematized. Instead Wenders concentrates on the creative sparks and devotion in the face of the master and the cloistral absorption of the women who work for him. The director of *Paris, Texas* and *Wings of Desire* transforms the Japanese formulation of the relation to alterity into an apotheosis of old European authority, a nostalgic masculine authorship, of the kind that the photographer and film-maker himself – one very last time, in the ongoing history of Romanticism – still hoped to be able to practice, in the face of the distorting image of the video camera.

Wenders proposes as a poetics for the inspirations of Yamamoto one of the most famous photographic projects in the studio of the master, August Sander's *Menschen des 20. Jahrhunderts*.[9] For Wenders – and here one cannot escape his viewpoint – these photographs represent in an exemplary way lost individuality – although Sander's intention was actually to establish an anthropological typology. Sander was searching for the universal element of a declining epoch, but his photographs have come to exemplify, in course of their modern reception, an inalienable individuality

– an identity of life form and expression, which Yamamoto's clothes seek to render. The late-Romantic Wenders sees such an identity in Sander, and wants to see it utopically realized in the clothes of Yamamoto. But the clothes of Yamamoto are less nostalgic than time-negating, anti-fashionable in a precise sense, and one that is characteristic of postfashion.

'I draw time' states 'Yohji' in the film, and he draws it into his clothes against the facelessness, the interchangeability of modern times. But what in the humble style of the monk of the middle ages, or in the worker and the petit bourgeois of Sander's photographs gives the impression of a timeless human life-form, as the glimpse of a possible better life, is only the after-image of a time which, anything but identical, now appears as the background of otherness. The ostensible poverty and plainness of this otherness, carrying humanity as driftwood, has a clear compensatory function in Yamamoto. Clothes which do not stand in the sign of luxury, of consumption and excess become beautiful by the fact of their sheer necessity. The model of elegance is not the dream woman of the West but the Russian working woman from a distant real world. 'Look at this warm coat. I would like to make something like that. You can see that she will use it. She will need it all the time to survive.' The moral of the story, however, which Wenders here has his Yohji communicate *via* the old photographs, is not the ill-concealed cynicism which would covertly steal from the poor of the past the only thing which they had left, the difficulty of surviving. Rather, an unsuspected irony lies in the strategy of Yamamoto, which lets poverty triumph as art, and thus accords it a discreet justice that the nostalgia of Wenders' film fails to reflect.

Jean-Paul Gaultier chose to present himself in the medium of a photo-novel, a genre which the popular press produces in a serial fashion for a readership that is primarily female, addicted to romance and on the run from reality. *A nous deux la mode* shows Gaultier's breathtaking parodic carnivalistic talent. 'Sa vie et son oeuvre,' the life and work as the model of the serious artist-monograph are made fun of from the first page, and with them, all the glossy magazines and luxurious coffee table books produced by his esteemed competitors. Not even the intellectually serious appeal of Rei Kawakubo's self-presentations or of Comme des Garçons avant-garde, private magazine *Six* could more radically reject the pretentions of the Paris fashion world.[10] In Gaultier's photo-novel, *haute couture* is made ridiculous in the distorting mirror of the petit bourgeois culture.

On the cover stands the happy smiling bride, radiant before a picture-book sky, with shining blue eyes and natural porcelain complexion, the bridal bouquet in her hand.[11] Gilles & Gilles quote with this trash photography the style of retouched portraits in the windows of small-town photography businesses. In the background stands the Eiffel Tower, the gilded tourist souvenir that decorates the plastic mantelpiece in the provinces. But then the impression is suddenly disrupted as with a closer look one sees that the bride is a man with a peroxide blonde crew cut, prominent ears, and a Breton striped T-shirt. Pudgy fingers hold the bouquet.

While Armani does his best to advertise the fact that his fashion is made for those who were born in flannel trousers, while Valentino emphasizes that his designs are meant for the happy few, while Yves Saint Laurent carefully demarcates himself from the street, in short, while all these designers underline that they work as better people for better people, Gaultier throws down the gauntlet to the aristocracy, to the bourgeoisie, to Paris. In the first place, he draws his inspiration from the street, in the second place, he does not lay claim to the creativity of genius. 'And where do you find all these new ideas?,' the *bon chic bon genre* journalist asks him with feigned innocence. 'From the street' comes the answer: 'I look around. It's not the couturiers who invent fashion: they just guess what the people want.' Moreover, the speaker here does not come from Avenue Montaigne, but from the suburbs, and indeed from the most petit bourgeois and unromantic of suburbs, namely from Arcueil, epitome of all musty suburban despair. The contrast is maintained as an ongoing commentary to the well-known *genre* of the dominant fashion houses. Where the designers of these houses have themselves photographed in palaces, villas or similarly luxurious surroundings, Gaultier chooses a dull apartment with flowered carpets and lace tray-cloths.

The ideology of the petit bourgeois is not spared by this virulent attack on the bourgeoisie. Costuming and gender-bending overcomes the paternal narrowness of petit bourgeois conformity. The little Jean-Paul plays like a girl with dolls, gives his teddy bear a make-over. He wants to become a hairdresser, a girl's job. Instead of going to school, he malingers, and spends the time with his grandmother, who runs a beauty salon in her living room. Early ideas are drawn from the trash. As the establishment says, the result is the *style poubelle*. His models are deliberately styleless, 'petits et ronds.' Not only does Gaultier use non-professional models, he is also one of the first designers to put old women and men on the catwalk. In a different way from Yamamoto, Gaultier leaves no place for Romantic misunderstandings. His fashion does not play with nostalgia; it has no compensatory characteristics. It is the present of the street, unreservedly positive in its view of its lowness, its poetry, and its inventiveness.

In the playful and not altogether coherent commentary, which tells of great heroic acts in the slipshod pathos of an Odyssey of fashion, success stands in the sign of disappointment, mastery in the sign of shoddy cutting:

> Tous écoutez cette complainte
> D'un garçon blond que l'on remarque
> Entre Tokyo et Central Park
> Et dont les robes désappointent
>
> C'est l'odyssée de la vêture
> Qui surgit des faubourgs d'Arcueil
> L'existence tout en clins d'oeil
> Du champion des entournures[12]

In contrast to the authentic signature of Yohji Yamamoto, the *griffe* of Gaultier is printed, easily misprinted, and the misprint reproducible at will. Gaultier knows that originality only comes into being through difference to the other designers, who all together construct the 'language' of fashion, the system of 'fashion': 'faut se faire remarquer.'

Notes

1. Roland Barthes, *The Fashion System*, trans. Matthew Ward and Richard Howard, Berkeley 1990. This classic of structural

analysis deals with fashion magazines between 1957 and 1963: it was originally published in Paris in 1967.

2. *Le Théâtre de la Mode* was shown in the Metropolitan Museum in New York in 1991.

3. Henry James, *The American*, New York 1981 (1867).

4. Yves Saint Laurent, *Images of Design 1958–1988*, with an introduction by Marguerite Duras, New York 1988, p. 229.

5. Jean-Paul Gaultier, *A nous deux, la mode*, Paris 1990.

6. This is the thesis of Richard Martin and Harold Koda, in *The Historical Mode – Fashion and Art in the 1980s*, New York 1989.

7. Pierre Schneider, in American *Vogue*, September 1976, p. 228.

8. As is especially impressively illustrated by the work of Issey Miyake; see, for instance, the exhibition 'Structure and Surface: Contemporary Japanese Textiles' at the Museum of Modern Art, New York 1999.

9. August Sander, *Menschen des 20. Jahrhunderts – Portrait- photographien 1892–1952*, ed. Gunther Sander, Munich 1980.

10. *Six*, ed. Atsuko Kozasu, No. 1–9, Tokyo 1988–91. Fashion seems incidental to the publication, with photography rather dominating. An exemplary motif: 'Sixth Sense,' No. 3, 1989.

11. See Bernarc Marcadé and Dan Cameron (eds), *Pierre & Gilles – The Complete Works*, Cologne 1997.

12. Gaultier, *A nous deux, la mode*.

Part II

Eight Types of Postfashion

The following analyses read clothes according to the parameters set up in the preceding chapters. Highlighting the formalistic aspects, the rhetorical figures, and the poetic procedures of designing, they proceed in a poetological manner, reading clothes the way one would read a poem for example. The readings focus on clothes and their relation to time, to gender clichés, and to class roles, and they explore their relationship to art and the politics of the *griffe*.

4

Lagerfeld for Chanel: The *Griffe*

Chanel under the direction of Karl Lagerfeld is the only house of *haute couture* and of *prêt-à-porter de luxe* which still has to figure in any discussion of the situation of fashion after the end of the 'century of fashion.' Under Lagerfeld, one sees a complete re-functionalization of the *griffe*, which had already long been more central to Chanel fashion than the clothes as such. The ongoing success of Chanel stems from a semiotic operation, invented by Lagerfeld, who signs, in a certain manner, in the name of Chanel, and makes this name into the centerpiece of Chanel fashion after Coco.

The *griffe*, the sign of the house, guarantees original authorial authenticity. It stands as the signature of the uniqueness, the inspiration and the ability of particular individuals. Traditionally, the *griffe* is hidden inside of the dress; it seals the contract between the couturier and the buyer. In *haute couture*, the *griffe* is the guarantee of a limited edition, and signifies the hands-on involvement of the master-designer. Through it, the fashion-creation approaches the artwork; it becomes a collector's object.

For the master, the *griffe* is the sign of his creative labor. For the buyer, it stands for his or her choice, the individuality of a taste, and as such, for that which, in the seventeenth and eighteenth centuries formed the aristocratic value *par excellence*: the cultivation of taste over time, that which would later be sublimated in the bourgeois concept of *Bildung*.

As a sign of non-codified individuality, the *griffe* contrasts with the heraldic emblem of inherited aristocratic privilege, but also with uniforms and traditional costumes serving to mark differences of rank or geographical region. Nonetheless, the 'individuality' which the *griffe* represents soon passes over into an emblematic function very close to that which the coat of arms once served. Louis Vuitton has his initials stamped into the travel bags that he sells; Chanel puts hers on the legendary suit buttons and pockets. The *griffe* is turned outwards and becomes a sign of prestige, documenting economic power rather than, as earlier, birth or taste. It no longer presumes any particular specialized knowledge, such as the cultivation of a sense of style; it can readily be deciphered by all – and, as soon became apparent, it can equally readily be counterfeited by all. As the insignia of the aristocracy of money, it is in a sense still an accreditation, a seal of genuineness, if only of the genuinely high price that has been paid for it.

The sale of the *griffe* soon became the greatest source of profits for the fashion houses. And although great commercial success was thereby achieved, a clearer symptom for the decline of Paris fashion, the 'mode de cent ans,' is hard to imagine. Licenses or royalties represent on average seven times the turnover brought into a fashion house by the clothes themselves: 68 percent of the turnover of Saint Laurent for example comes from royalties. The *griffe* passes from being an index, in the semiotic sense, which guarantees an almost physical relation to the designer, to being an arbitrary sign, which can be legally bought and sold – and also illegally. Significantly, Chanel, in pronounced contrast to some other design houses, has maintained a relatively restricted licensing policy (only 3 percent of the turnover).

Where, in the time of Coco Chanel, fashion designers insisted on a legally protected copyright for their creations, today it is the *griffe* that is protected. Chanel herself did not support her colleagues in their hopeless battle to retain the copyright of their creations – i.e., in their attempts to control the proliferation of copying and modification of their work – even though her work was copied extensively, and not only by the mass-production lines, but also by the other designers. The reason for this is clear and radical: if it is true that fashion destroys itself in the moment of its realization, the copy can only be a misunderstanding. Fashion is virtuality: it uses up all its magic in the moment of its actualization, and in the same moment begins to decline and age. Chanel held to the radicality of this insight, and, over the longer period, the market confirmed her judgment. The claim of Chanel's idea of fashion (as transmitted by Paul Morand) is not that the copy authenticates the originality of the original. It is that the original simply cannot be copied, because it destroys itself, because it does not attain to any lasting identity in time. Morand recalls by way of anecdote:

> I remember an evening at Ciro's where there were 17 Chanel dresses, none of them from the House of Chanel. The Duchess d'Albe greeted me with these words: 'I swear to you that mine really comes from Chanel.' And [then also] this narration of the Duchesse de La Rochefoucauld who responded to a friend who she had invited along with me: 'I do not dare to meet her, my Chanel dress is not from her.' And I answered 'I am not certain if my own clothes come from my house.'[1]

Fashion exhibits a protean power of creation, a pure potency of genius, which, like Phoenix, constantly rises anew out of the ashes. As dead, it attests only to the living. In face of the success of the innumerable copies, the original Chanel rises indestructible. But the same could not be said with respect to the symbol of the house, the signature 'Chanel,' which comes to compensate for what has been lost at the level of fashion and innovation. Postfashion is fashion after and against Chanel. It remakes fashion from the start, and conceives of itself by way of its opposition to the commercial success that Chanel (and similar companies) manage to achieve by giving up on fashion. Chanel-fashion now lives entirely from the *griffe*, from the 'predator's claw' (the literal meaning of *griffe*), a predator in this case that specializes in money and that plays with the death-drive of those who have too much of it, and nothing else.

Today, Chanel sells nothing other than its *griffe*; the *griffe* is an absolute symbol for 'fashion' which, having become historical, is now able to sell this history better than it could sell fashion. Chanel's lasting success proves that fashion has become self-referential: the fetish of the mere name shows how it has begun to revolve around itself. The House of Chanel produces what Coco most abhorred: a thing of the past, dead. The visible, outwardly displayed *griffe* has become the opposite of individualized style: instead it confirms the latent uniform collectivity, which had always defined Chanel-wear; in the end, it signifies membership of an expensive club. The Chanel woman does not want to display her own taste, she wants to belong. In order to be certain, she is laden with Chanel signs and accessories, like amulets to protect against the evil eye; on the pocket, on the belt, on the dress buttons, on the watch, on costume jewelry, proudly stand the initials of the founder of the house, to which she knows she belongs. In the winter collection of 1991/2 there prevailed such an *esprit réclame* that even the most non-expert eye could have no doubt that this was Chanel-fashion. The name Chanel was printed on T-shirts in large letters, and towels were covered with advertising copy such as 'I love Coco.' The French newspaper *Libération* commented that the brand-marking in this *défilé* had taken on the proportions of buffalo-rearing in the Wild West.

The *prêt-à-porter de luxe* has long made the transition to imitating the marketing of a wider sector of the *sentier*; Benetton and Gap, Chevignon and Lacoste display their labels as prominently as possible, as if to sell their clothing as advertising for their logos, just as sporting teams sell the logos of their sponsors. In Chanel boutiques, the same youth-group mentality dominates, the same blind devotion to symbols. One could hardly conceive of a more grotesque spectacle than the Chanel store in the legendary rue Cambon, where women dressed as girls in blue and white school uniforms with pleated skirts – all from Chanel of course – supply well-to-do foreign tourists with the famous monogram.

The style of the collections themselves has developed into a loose assortment of all that is popularly associated, under the name of Chanel, with 'fashion.' Certainly, Lagerfeld does not do what one would tend to expect from a designer – namely to project a particular style. What appears on the catwalk is only too familiar. The show becomes an experiment in *déjà-vu*, without surprises. Popular fashion recycled *chez* Chanel. In the first place, the house naturally cites itself and its own past contributions to fashion: the Chanel suit which, even when it comes in washed-out denim, in pink wool-crêpe with black or white crumple-trimming, or in lurex with silver-gleaming fringes, remains ever what it always was. The 1960s come again in candy-colored artificial pastels and even color the hair of the models, adorned with glittering tinsel, to create an effect reminiscent of Christmas decoration.

The signs of the time point to cheap kitsch. All kinds of past styles and fashions pass in colorful revue: the tulle skirt and ballerina shoes, a little Western style, a little sado-maso, lots of silver zippers, black leather and associated uniform fantasies, a little Hells Angels and motorcycle sex, a little tropical look, a little *bleu/blanc bon chic bon genre, croisière* and Deauville, a little Spanish folklore with torero sequins, some forest and nature nymphs with plastic jewelry, the undershirt of the teenager. The classic style-citations of the fashion scene pile up confusedly: Mugler-style comic creatures, the genital-covering ivy of Vivienne Westwood, the pointed tails of Romeo Gigli. The mannequins swing between little girl, child-woman and strange doll-like transvestite. But what is here being shown, staged and, in the end, also sold is not clothes, nor is it a particular taste or a personal predilection: it is the all-powerful guarantee of a brand name which has become a mythical signifier for fashion: above all else, the intertwined CC of the founder Chanel. Where his legendary predecessor created fashions and was copied, Lagerfeld has reversed the process: no longer a forerunner or trendsetter, he copies fashion *après coup*, and then authenticates it through the *griffe*.

Fashion copies used to appear under a false name and sought to pass themselves off as genuine. Now the copy has its own label, a *griffe* which signifies this process of copying the copy, of authenticating fakes: Chanel. Since the *griffe*, in the copy as in the fake, remains the only thing which is genuine, it can even copy its own copies, authenticate the counterfeits of itself. What Chanel sells as genuine are copies of the counterfeits of 'genuine' Chanels which street traders offer in poorer quality and at a fraction of the price. The only thing which is genuine and interesting about all this is the dissolution of the categories of genuine and fake that it accomplishes. Chanel's methods mirror the structure of a market whose ironies have become vertiginous. One of these ironies is that Chanel itself fails to see them. Chanel

USA now litigates at great expense, over long periods of time, and without notable success, against the faking of the *griffe* whose very counterfeitability has assured the company's success. In New York, one comes across this *griffe* constantly in the stalls of street traders, for sale at the lowest prices. Presumably unaware how exactly they had hit the nail on the head, the New York authority responsible for counterfeits commented to the *Village Voice* that it was starting to seem as if the whole New York market consisted of nothing but counterfeits: *très à propos* Chanel, who sell the copy of a fake as an original. The plastic rose with the *signum* of Chanel has become more genuine than the original rose ever was.

Chanel no longer makes *haute couture*: rather, it brings *haute couture* definitively to an end, galvanizes it like a dead body. For Yves Saint Laurent, even in the most exotic of citations, it was still primarily a matter of creating an individual style, of authenticating his fashion. And while Laurent signs, with his naked flawed (bespectacled) body, and in flesh and blood, Karl Lagerfeld disappears behind dark glasses, stylizing himself as a Don Juan of the eighteenth century. He transforms Chanel into a hyperbolic pastiche of *haute couture*. He does not merely produce kitsch, he also shows that what he makes is kitsch. Fashion becomes an over-priced costume drama, driven by the ghost of what it once was. Lagerfeld seeks less to appropriate this empty aura than to reflect its emptiness. The less-informed customer who can still be dazzled by this uncanny glamour, who wants to buy the past that is being conjured up, sees in an empty reflection the sensory representation of abstract money.

At the end of fashion, this fashion has become a ready-made, fashion from a can. It has become an empty formula, which means nothing but the predicate '*haute couture*' and the reproduction at will of any given style, without regard for its content. Lagerfeld could produce pastiches incognito for any of the fashion houses whose style has hardened into formula (such as Gucci, Givenchy and Valentino). His individuality lies in the renunciation of individuality. Assuming the same aura of the creative artist that Worth had earlier borrowed from Rembrandt, he exhibits his products as fakes, a *Bouvard et Pécuchet* of the contemporary fashion world.

Moschino is the symmetrical counterpart to Chanel. He shares with Chanel a certain uniformity of style, aimed at winning popular appeal. Both are characterized by a pleasant, almost crude reliance on the appeal of gender and class clichés. These schemata have to be recognizable, decodable even, on a first glance. There is neither place nor time for subtleties, for concealed, intimate features sewn into the dress, of which only the wearer is aware. With their bold, simplistic effects both Chanel and Moschino borrow something from the strategies of pop art and the *esprit réclame*. Chanel transforms these strategies, shining the golden radiance of the *griffe* on to relatively trivial ideas and elevating them into the sky of high fashion and elegance; Moschino applies the opposite strategy, drawing high fashion, the symbol of luxury, downwards, and making it compatible with pop culture. 'Chic and cheap' is the title of a collection by Moschino. On the back of an otherwise unremarkable tweed jacket, one sees emblazoned in golden letters: THIS IS AN EXPENSIVE JACKET. Where Lagerfeld surrounds vulgarity with the breath of Chanel elegance, Moschino makes money by vulgarization. Lagerfeld is able to sell a denim jacket for 4,000 dollars, Moschino for at least 400 dollars, and no doubt ten times more often.

Moschino could hardly have found a finer object for the vulgarization process than Chanel. And, of course, it had to come to litigation: in one of the most famous cases in fashion law, Chanel sued Moschino, not for the copy of a design, but for the sake of the prestige of the *griffe*. It was not a matter of the illegal application of the trademark label, but of a parodic misuse: a suit made out of knitted ribbons, and designed, of course, by Moschino himself. The symbolic capital of Chanel, its lifeblood, was more dangerously threatened by parody than by the tried and true process of copying copies.

Note

1. Paul Morand, *L'allure de Chanel*, Paris 1976, p. 141.

5

Montana, Mugler: Myth

'Back to the future' could be the motto of the Mugler or Montana – back to the future of science fiction. Every woman can be a superwoman, a streamlined super-feminine warrior, landed from outer space. The source of this fashion is the new female body invented in comic books. The feminine body is programmed, down to the least gestures: emphatic curves – breast, bottom, waist, leg – controlled by a strong muscle-tone; the whole goes hand in hand with a sharply defined set of movements, composed of a free mixture of pornographic postures and military drill.

The individual body, with its frailties and imperfections, is eclipsed by the idealizing mimesis of the suit. This mimesis remains nonetheless 'idealistic': it aggressively models the so-called secondary sexual characteristics, imitating the exaggerated femininity of Barbie dolls. The phallic woman, mythically inviolable and perfect, is its guiding image. Mugler and Montana draw on the reservoir of submerged mythology, now most recognizable and accessible in the form of the comic books, with their invincible heroes. The heroes of modernity, congealed into clichés, are hyper-realistically imitated: in the background stand Mussolini's vision of imperial splendor, the larger-than-life superwomen of the revolutionary Soviet Union, the epic strength of the heroes of social realism, and American 'Star Wars' fantasies.

The sharply outlined compact silhouette is the center around which everything revolves. Vision is granted an exclusive privilege over the sense of touch: the simplified silhouette can be taken in at one glance. The modeling of the body by the suit is meant to subtract the fabric and the body from the effects of time, of fading, of the play of light on the material, even from the effects of movement and from unpredictable individual deviations from the ideal body-norm. The suggestion is of the invincibility of the perfect plastic body. The clothes feature gleaming metallic zips that open in one gliding movement or press-studs that click open and shut with automatic precision. Serge Gainsbourg's 'Comic-strip girl' comes to mind: 'bang, pow, whizz': thus speaks the Mugler woman, with marked American accent.

The exaggeration of the silhouette is accomplished by solid fabrics or with leather – materials that do not fall, but maintain their tension. This quality of the material is enhanced by a sophisticated cutting technique. The stitching itself underlines the tendency of the cut, especially in Mugler's work; the seams are narrow between breast and waist, for example, so that the lines heighten the effect of the cut, making the waist slimmer and the breasts larger. The uniformity of the body created in this way is emphasized by the use of single colors – artificial, open colors, which convey no suggestion of vulnerability – and materials which allow no irregularities to appear. Skirt and jacket are created from the same material and in the same color, presenting a uniform surface in defiance of contrary fashion-trends, such as the wild mixes of patterns and materials introduced by Lacroix. The body of the woman in this outfit is naively phallic: a super-feminine textile body, a smooth, impenetrable and flawless form offers itself to the gaze.

6

Dolce & Gabbana: Deep South

Dolce & Gabbana have followed the classic Italian trek, from the south to the north, the same way taken by the impoverished farm-workers from Sicily who became industrial proletariat in Turin and Milan. This path has left its mark on the clothes they create: from the clerical institutions and Sicilian country-life, from peasant girls and the legendary queens of the Middle Ages, the fashion of Dolce & Gabbana has proceeded to the early industrial, early capitalist proletariat. The reservoir of images on which they draw comes from sources such as cheap vaudeville, costumed performing girls, the nebulous fringes of the *bohème*, the genteel poverty of the ruined bourgeoisie, governesses and teachers and also, of course, the workers, in the style of films of Rossellini. In all of this, there is a touch of Sicilian passion, in the manner of Sophia Loren: an affirmative, even aggressive feminine eroticism, adult and dominant.

Within Italian fashion, Dolce & Gabbana started as *enfants terribles*. French fashion has always had a tendency towards the experimental, and has striven for the surprising, and the certain something, the 'je ne sais quoi.' Italian fashion, on the other hand, has tended to confine itself to ideals of beauty and classical harmony. It aims more to perfectly fulfill the norms than to introduce innovations – hence its success in the conservative German market.

Dolce & Gabbana, on the other hand, prefer rhetorical figures, ironic and parodic citations that could never and are not supposed to appear natural, but rather deliberately emphasize social indices and produce stark disharmonies. Their target was nostalgic, sentimental fashion. The theatrical coats in red faded velvet, trimmed with pieces of tapestry showing hunting scenes, and the enormous brocade jackets from the 1990 winter collection did not conjure up the charm of a bygone era, but rather deconstructed its sentimentality and raided it for citations. In their caricatural exaggeration, it is less the perfume of the past that was recalled than its oppressive atmosphere. Instead of looking like a medieval queen, the wearer looked like a modern woman who wanted to disguise herself as a comic-book medieval queen; impatiently she waited for the horse to be bridled so she could gallop off into the distance. Likewise, the black capes made out of fine wool felt (winter collection 1991) called to mind less the *humilitas* of the clergy than their addiction to finery: they were decorated, moreover, and very advantageously, with a luxurious multicolored silk-crêpe bow. The range of Italian citations also includes nuns' and monks' habits, priests' and bishops' garments. The doubled black clerical cassock from Momento Due in Milan rejects all false sentimentality through its discreet arrogance, and signals the irony of its all-but-pious idleness in the buttonhole: a hunting green loden-citation reveals the pastoral vocation as feudal hunting-life in another form.

Figure 4 shows a dress from the winter collection of 1989/90, which is made from a fine wool-jersey. In contrast with the close-fitting top, a skirt made out of four diagonally cut lengths of material hangs in soft folds that follow the body with every movement and swings widely over the ankles. The technique of diagonal cutting, introduced into *haute couture* by Madeleine Vionnet, is here decisive. The technique is invisible, lending a very natural appearance to the improbably soft fall, creating an unbelievable suppleness in the material. The top, which is cut like a T-shirt with round collar-ending, contains the upper-body snugly. The jacket, likewise close-fitting, continues the

Figure 4
Dolce & Gabbana, 1989–90,
© Steel Stillman.

wrapping of the body down to the legs. In another invisible technique, the jacket is cut out of the same piece of material as the dress underneath, such that the one piece is drawn over the other without any intervening space. From this secret doubling, the impression of greater softness as well as greater fluidity is created: soft, flexible, slim and yet luxurious.

This doubleness, whereby finely knitted wool materials or even blouses are drawn the one over the other, is a constant feature of Dolce & Gabbana, and makes for a neat allegory on their name as well. It also serves to bring the breasts into a favorable light, an ongoing concern of this pair of designers.

In this case, the jacket is done up under the breasts with flat smooth matt-black buttons, to underline the classical, minimal impression. Everything in this outfit has to be adjusted and straightened up; a few buttons remain open: all kinds of little folds are formed. The jacket is counter-lined, and – here too, the impression is of an effect of chance – the stitches of this counter-lining are turned upwards, to create a slight three-dimensionality, sliding and smooth, changing with the movement of the body. Underneath, set in the *decolleté*, the breasts, preferably alabaster white, palely shimmer through. When it is a matter of neck, breasts, upper arm, or *decolleté*, no-one can hold a candle to Dolce & Gabbana. These body parts are framed with inimitable beauty; from the close-fitting fabrics, gathered into little folds, the woman emerges like Venus from the foam.

The strict governness look seems to be tempered with an element of slight disorder, and, through this suggestion of disorder alone, gains an erotic overtone. That which in the style of the governness has a certain uniform-character, with something also of the suffragette, and which is calculated to achieve a total desexualization is here eroticized by means of small modelings in the cut. From the technical point of view, these are very advanced, and require the greatest application. The degree of eroticization accomplished is so much the more remarkable, in that it comes across as inconspicuous. The conflict takes place entirely at the level of what is implicit and unspoken. The semiotics of the most resolute hostility to sexuality is quietly transformed into its opposite.

The mastery of the craftmanship is apparent in the way that all this has an altogether individual and natural air, as if the eroticization were an effect of chance. This is one of the most successful of Dolce & Gabbana's creations, precisely because of the double register at which the language of fashion is here made to operate. It respects the conventions and the demands of suffragette–governness clothing, with its black unpretentious cloth, the high-necked form, the covering of the legs, the careful concealment of all erotic parts of the body. It renounces jewelry, is sober and rigorous – and yet brings out like scarcely any other the eroticism of the feminine body. And it goes to show that this eroticism lies in the multiple modes of veiling and disguising.

The extent of the influence of the punk movement, raised into the sky of high fashion in the shape of Vivienne Westwood, can be measured by the fact that cheap refuse materials like plastic and lurex, in vulgar patterns such as tiger and leopard-skin, have made their way into the Chanel collection. With them a new eroticism has entered the scene. 'Sado-maso' and the many forms of sexual fetishism, which were introduced into street fashion by the punk scene, brought the traditional concepts of body and clothing, sex and the erotic, into disarray. Even sexy underwear showed itself amenable to integration, and it was in its sign that Dolce & Gabbana were to triumph. Dolce & Gabbana's irony, which owed much to the aggressivity of the punk scene, brings out the almost lost erotic potential of ostentatious intimacy, in that they once again allow underwear to be underwear.

In strident disharmony, expensive corsages, trimmed over and over with pearls, rhinestone and paste, of the kind that grace only the largest evening-wear wardrobes, combine and clash with bra-straps such as one would probably still only be able to find in small out-of-the-way market towns in East Europe and Sicily. Long elegant evening-gloves are worn with a rather simple bra. Insignia of power, insignia of elegance and insignia of porno appear side by side. Images of luxury and images of cheap pornography reveal disconcerting affinities. Under a splendid cloak of fake leopard-skin, luxuriously lined with red velvet, a red velvet corsage comes into view. The elegance of a gossamery silk material in an exquisite color is combined with the crudest straps. Feathers vacillate between pretentious evening-wear trimmings à la Givenchy and cheap erotic underwear. One sees here easily what is influencing and what is being influenced.

Dolce & Gabbana's underwear look became most famous through the long-running 'girdle-motif,' which even adorned the cover of *Vogue Italia*, but which was naturally a flop in humorless and prudish America. In many variations – sleeveless, with braces, in combination with a fine long-sleeved wool-jersey, as a skirt with a two-piece jersey top, or as a simple top – it has become something like a trademark of the firm. With this emblem, too, the principle of doubling is maintained: the material of the girdle is doubled with a black, brownish or faded violet-black wool material. And it is no accident that it was this motive that brought the irony of the house its triumph.

In the 1960s and 1970s underwear was the epitome of the private and the intimate, of that which is hidden and banned from the public sphere. In the decades which followed it saw a change in its fortunes, becoming not only socially presentable but also the solitary star of the fashion scene. Wearing underwear as overwear was one of the most popular fashion trends of the period, enjoying success in a number of variations. On the one hand, the trend involved a revitalization and extension of the kind of carefully staged and exhibited eroticism, such as has always existed in semi-public spaces. Luxury eroticism rediscovered the boudoir look, reminiscent of the coquette of the eighteenth century, with lots of lace, tulle, and the wonderfully colorful luminous silks that *Jeune Europe* brought to perfection. The furor for *corsages* conjured up associations with a tradition in feminine underwear that had been long dormant, and recalled the ball gowns and great evening-wear wardrobes of the nineteenth century, with its hothouse eroticism. It evoked the women in novels, from Balzac to Zola, who, with their shimmering alabaster shoulders, their silk and lace, their pearls and diamonds, stand out so strikingly from the dark matt-colored masculine background. Less expensive versions, derived from street prostitution, also turned up, with garter belts worn over stockings and lots of patent leather, often parodically punked up. The Hollywood Glamor Girl with fringes, sequins, precious stones, feathers and paste-jewelry was a third variant. Jean-Paul Gaultier's bustiers, surrealistic artworks, are an ironic aesthetization of this tendency, reflecting on the sublimation of the body which had first to have taken place, for it to be possible that underwear could be 'discovered.'

At the same time that the semi-private was released from its narrowly restricted sphere and allowed to make its way onto the public stage of everyday life, there was an attempt to eliminate the intimate-private aspect from non-erotic underwear. Designers produced shirts that could also be worn as T-shirts, under-shorts that could also be worn as shorts; even in underwear, one is still dressed. In Calvin Klein's functional fitness aesthetic, the intimate, with its embarrassing aspect, is definitively suppressed. Or rather, a new way of suppressing it is discovered: the body, made healthy, functional and ready-to-go by aerobics and jogging, with a fortified sex-appeal – lightly tanned, thoroughly washed, properly nourished, muscular and controlled – can let itself be seen in all situations. Well depilated, it really has nothing to hide: it is not a secret, shameful body, but rather a public, successful body, shorn of all possibilities of old-European eroticism.

Dolce & Gabbana, on the other hand, rejoin a tradition in underwear which neither stages a constructed erotic for the public gaze, nor antiseptically presents a desexualized sport-body. It produces the shock of the intimate-private in unmodified form, and is decidedly not presentable in public. The origin in bygone provincial fashion, the citation of a past proletariat and petit bourgeois milieu, is unmistakable. At one stroke what Heine had to say about hidden Trieste beauty, and what Sophia Loren brought on to the screen – a specific erotic national wealth – is reawakened. The shock that it causes is a reminder of what underwear was before it abandoned the sphere of the precariously intimate and the embarrassingly private. Precisely in the reversal of the official eroticism, the garment gains a new and completely different erotic charge. In the first place, the erotic connotations are toned down by the minimalism and pauperism of the piece, by its complete simplicity – unadorned, authentic down to the eyelets and the cheap nylon, it really evokes nothing other than a girdle. On the other hand, the eroticism of the piece is intensified and sublimated by the fact that it is designed for a body that needs no such instrument of correction, and that leaves the corrective function far behind. What was already known from *Oggi ieri Domani*, namely that a luxurious beauty overwhelms the girdle no less effectively than the girdle holds in a declining body, now becomes a provocation. This girdle should loosely clothe a slim, almost thin, elegance. Only by its absolute functionlessness can the shock of the article pass over into aesthetic pleasure. The complex and sophisticated art through which the feminine body was formerly produced, and which had above all to remain secret in order to lend the body a naturally attractive appearance – the functional supports, reinforcements, double seams, the elastic or inelastic material – is now openly exhibited. At the same moment, however, that the elements of this art lose their function, they are already beginning to transform into a flattering and ironic adornment. The secret means of containment become the signs of a newly acquired freedom.

7

Comme des Garçons:
Ex Oriente Lux

When Rei Kawakubo presented her first show in Paris in 1981 an outcry went through the international press, such as no other designer has elicited. The indignation responded to what was perceived as an attack on the idea of fashion in general, and on the ideal of the 'Western woman' in particular – in short, an attack on beauty. This critical counter-attack was carried out with an aggressivity which did not balk at a cynical and tactless use of national and sexist stereotypes. In the USA, the press of the nation that had dropped the atom bombs on Japan was not above disparaging remarks about a 'post-atom-bomb-fashion,' marked by death, tattered shrouds, depression, destruction, poverty and hunger. Traumatized by the defeat in the war, the Japanese, it seemed, were unable to take pleasure in their newly acquired wealth, and now opposed the triumph of the new world order with an enigmatic obstinacy.

If one recalls that this new aesthetic of poverty was attacked in America at the same time that the nation was being drawn down into Third World conditions by the percentage of the population living in poverty, then it is tempting to wonder if what was at issue here was less the victory in the Second World War than the defeat in the economic war. Certainly, the economic triumph of post-war Japan is in no way celebrated in Kawakubo's designs – herein lies perhaps the deepest provocation of Comme des Garçons, in Japan as in America. An American power elite, which holds undeterred to the ostentatious exhibition of Western values through wealth and consumption, could only view with consternation a designer who makes a New York bag lady into a new fashion ideal. Meanwhile, as carefully as the media try to conceal it, the conflict between rich and poor is visible for all to see on the street, and not only there where one is accustomed not to look, but also where one is compelled to look, namely in the provocations of postfashion.

The European press was perhaps more tactful, but not more receptive. Kawakubo was a woman who created fashion 'as men do,' and iconoclastically transgressed one of the unwritten laws of Western culture: she questioned the monopoly of the French in matters of elegance, and the expertise of French *couture*. Worse yet, she had begun to challenge the dearest-held belief of this culture, the pillar that holds the whole social order in place: the social construction of the 'woman,' as the beautiful, graceful gender. Already with the name of her label, Comme des Garçons, Kawakubo dedicated herself to precisely that which women were not allowed to be.

The questioning of the institution of fashion was also under-taken, and very successfully, at the more technical level. The black pullovers of her so-called Lace Collection were strewn at random with small holes, as if they had been attacked by an army of moths. The European fashion press could see in this nothing but an allegory of mortality: of the decadence and decomposition of Western fashion itself. In any case, these clothes were certainly not ignored. The powerful use of black made the bright splendor of the other collections seem completely colorless in comparison; the ingenious asymmetries and loose overlays of the fabric branded ideas of the perfect cut, the absolute line and the flawless execution as relics of another day; and the holes in the fabric furnished an ironic commentary on the sophisticated arts of embroidery and lace-making.

Rei Kawakubo could not have been too unhappy about this reception. After all, such massed indignation is the traditional response to avant-garde artworks, even their accreditation in a certain sense. Through the shock and resistance, the explosive novelty, the originality and the radicality of the artist is confirmed. Comme des Garçons was soon taken up into the realm of art. The Lace Collection of 1981 has become part of the collection of the Victoria and Albert Museum in London, photographs of the show have been exhibited in the Beaubourg in Paris, and in 1987 an exhibition was devoted to Kawakubo's work, along with that of two other designers, at the New York Fashion Institute of Technology. Rei Kawakubo undoubtedly stands in the tradition of the avant-garde movements of classical modernity. She has been strongly influenced by movements such as Bauhaus, by its heroes such as Le Corbusier, and even by its treasured concepts such as the *tabula rasa*: the idea of beginning again from zero, often repeated by the designer, is characteristic. Like the avant-gardes, Kawakubo sets the functionality of the line against the merely decorative, and hence superficial, ornament. And with the classical avant-garde she shares an aversion to the very core of fashion: the production of beautiful appearance, which she exposes as such. The shock that Kawakubo's work provokes is in fact not primarily the social shock; this latter is rather a secondary effect. Her aesthetic is, in the end, not an aesthetic of poverty, even if much of the provocative effect of her work comes from this direction. Rather it is a negative aesthetic, based in a contestation of the idea of fashion itself.

Kawakubo's negative aesthetic, as Harold Koda has shown, is marked by the ascetic ideals of Zen Buddhism, such as it was developed in the sixteenth and seventeenth centuries in reaction to the protocol, ceremony and ostentatiousness of court life. But in the West, too, poverty as sparsity, as an aesthetic category opposed to the luster and false appearances of the idle world, and related ideals, such as ascesis, self-sufficiency, freedom from desire, and isolation from the distraction and confusion of society, are not entirely new. In the early Modern period of the Ancien Régime, the anti-aesthetic of the Parisian religious reform-movement, Port-Royal, laid the foundations for an aesthetic appreciation of poverty, of age, of the marks of use, of coldness and darkness, of decline – in short, of the non-beautiful as such, seen as making legible the traces of a truth that is white-washed over by the ideal of beauty: the truth of the fallenness and mortality of the only apparently beautiful world. Comme des Garçons, as well as the response that Kawakubo's work provoked, take us back into this pre-history of European fashion, summoning up the radicality of a renunciation of worldiness that had subsequently been erased from the memory of fashion. It may be correct, in this respect, as the Japanese fashion-historian Kazuko Koike has argued, that Kawakubo draws on the charisma of religious movements.

In the Western topology, fashion is the epitome of (false) beautiful appearance, of the empty vanity of this world. Clothing – in opposition to veils, which cover over a truth that is to be unveiled – is the metaphor of deceptive rhetoric itself. Like the mask, but less openly, which is to say, more deceptively, clothing hides, disguises and travesties the essence. Clothes make the man, as the saying goes: into something that he is not, glosses the moral and philosophical tradition. Kawakubo is remarkable in that she does not see fashion as subject to a logic of appearance and disguise, but rather in the sign of a fragile identity. Her innovation is that she does not disguise: her clothes let the inner shine through, or at least, make it in general possible that something like inwardness can be communicated. As one impressed reviewer put it, Kawakubo does not see clothes as a means of influencing others, or even as a medium for self-presentation; rather, her clothes serve to heighten one's own well-being, and should reflect one's own thinking.

Western reformulations tend to remain at the level of an either/or opposition, according to which the outer covering has to let the inner truth be seen; therefore, the body, especially the deceptive and seductive feminine body, has to be made to disappear. Kawakubo's comments refer rather to a balance in which inner and outer are to be maintained. And, naturally, this can then be vulgarized and sold to an American public along the lines of the slogan, 'be what you are.' Entirely in the line of the puritanical tradition, it is the suppression of sexuality and sensuality in Kawakubo's clothing which is then seen to be essential. Similarly, the refined technique of multiple layering is seen purely as a means of discouraging any kind of 'peekaboo' voyeurism. Certainly, it is true that the particular erotics of clothing referred to by Roland Barthes as the rhetoric of the right gaps is not at work here. The erotic topics of Western fashion are indeed negated. What remains after this, however, is not nothing, and is certainly not an indifference to the claims of the body. In Kawakubo's clothing, the Western fashion-world is confronted with a different way of reading the body. In place of the dialectic of concealing and revealing, and the conventions of sexuality and sensuality derived from this dialectic, there emerges a sensuality of changing silhouettes, layered in the depths of the fabric. The conventionality that lies in the background and informs the play of the silhouettes has to remain foreign to us. But the altogether sensory impact of the clothing is only the more visible for this. Rarely has an inter-cultural contextual displacement so immediately exposed an aesthetic potential.

Jean-Paul Gaultier has wittily showed up sexual bravado as the core of Western fashion. An essential moment of this bravado is the division of the body into fetish-like partial objects, and the enlargement and isolation of particular parts: breast, waist, foot, etc. In order to be exhibited in and for itself, the freedom of movement of the particular part has to be limited; at the same time a whole mechanics is created (how does one sit down while wearing a short, tight skirt?), in order to keep the contrast of concealment and revealing operational. Against such an erotically staged corporeality, Kawakubo posits a body which is not exhibited to the gaze, but rather protected, allowed to remain whole and moveable. Hence, Comme des Garçons, as part of its self-differentiation from Western fashion, takes as its emblem the classical torso, from which rises an intact figure. This figure is characterized by a different kind of eroticism, one which deconstructs the Western opposition of naked and clothed, and promotes in its place a symbiosis of body and clothing. This fashion is indeed strongly physical; it does not, however, treat the body as an object, to be exhibited, but instead as something that is one's own, that belongs to and with the inner self. Kawakubo does not aim for a spiritualization or a concealment of the body, but rather for a new mode of embodiment. The relative indeterminateness of the clothing, which leaves a great deal of freedom to the wearer, corresponds to this intention. There is always scope for adjustment and variation, according to one's preferences. Often, the articles are reversible, and have no definite right or left side. Or, in an ironization of their own principle: one slips into a first sleeve, then into a second, only to discover yet a third sleeve, which lets the first pass through it, and hints at an infinitization of the dressing process.

Comme des Garçons was one of the first labels to have consistently cultivated the reduction of the commodity character of their work as a marketing strategy. Early on, Rei Kawakubo had devised a kind of advertising which refrained from exhibiting the commodity as such, a move which was to be determining for the whole industry. The thing itself, the commodity as object of acquisitive desire, is only indirectly present, signaled in the background. In the foreground is a particular atmosphere – for Comme des Garçons, that of the European avant-gardes of the 1920s and 1930s, of the photography of Kertéz, for example. In the layout of its stores, Comme des Garçons seeks to avoid appearing as an outlet for commodities. All post-modern overtones notwithstanding, the display spaces are in the spirit of the International style. Each store is individually designed for the city in which it is located. Even the furniture is designed by Kawakubo. The small number of garments occupying a large space creates the effect of a gallery rather than a store – a museum, in which one can just as well come to contemplate the artworks as to buy something. 'Sublime Body Parts' is the only outward sign of her latest shop in Chelsea, New York, a former garage, the only clothing shop in the midst of a row of galleries.

As an alternative to a fashion press which offers scarcely more than an upscale mail-order catalogue, Comme des Garçons' magazine, *Six*, avoids 'ideological words and tangible goods.' The magazine is very fine, superbly put together and with many interesting ideas. It is concerned with structures and principles, with Kawakubo's modernism, and not with her clothes. The clothes are rather one element among others, one form of an ongoing experimentation with style. A polemic runs throughout against consumerism and tourism; correspondingly, there is an existentialist-style praise of marginal existences, of the poor who live on the edges of the city, in areas which decidedly do not belong to the fashion world. There is praise too for the exceptional, simple individuals, those who are able to enjoy the simple joys, whose luxury is authenticity, and who therefore have an elective affinity with those who live on the margin of society. The problem of the consumer society is explicitly posed in terms of life-philosophy, and not in terms of class.

In striking contrast to the obsession with genius characteristic of the fashion world, and its concomitant deadly competitiveness, not only other artists, but also other designers show together with Kawakubo: Alaia and Miyake, for example, alongside Lindberg and Enzo Cucchi, Dino Buzzati and John Cale, Francesco

Clemente and Dennis Hopper, appear as rescuing angels of a society losing itself in empty consumerism. The longing after the authentic which these figures embody can, in semiotic terms, be expressed as a desire for the indexical sign. And some collections from Comme des Garçons are interspersed with such indices, amulet-like signs of ethnic authenticity, hand-weaved Indian fabrics, on which the traces of time and the touch of the individual human hand are there to be read, sewed in to the cloth. Earlier in her career, Kawakubo would loosen screws, in order to restore irregularities and flaws to the perfection of machine-made products. Ten years later, she was no longer satisfied with such simulacra of handicraft. The simulacrum provoked anew the longing for the original, created 'the original' anew. Thus it is the commodity which gives birth to the desire for the absence of the commodity, and, under this sign, celebrates its greatest triumph.

One's first impression is of an early baroque classicism. Through a distantiating reinterpretation of antiquity, the design shown in Figure 5 recounts the history of the Western perversion of the erotic. In reverting to antique models and in rewriting their reception, the relation of nakedness and dress, of fabric and body, appears in a new light. *Ex oriente lux*: the Western interpretations, imitations and classicisms of every kind are placed in the shade by the distant Japanese sun. Never have the moderns been able to reproduce the apparently effortless sculptural accomplishments of the ancients. From hard, cold, heavy stone came soft, light, transparent veils, and from out of these falling folds, the appearance of vital, living flesh imposes itself. The stone as veil first discloses the flesh as really naked and living. Here there is no trace of the marmoreal hardness, stone-cold opacity, lifeless whiteness, 'chaste,' frozen nakedness, such as one finds in all the classicisms, before and after Canova. In antiquity, through the working of the stone, flesh becomes perceptible as the opposite of stone. In classicism, by contrast, flesh is transformed into stone. The classicist fashions of the Second Empire and of the 1920s make women into statues, who always retain something of the statue's marble chastity, even when unclothed. Vionnet's 'Wrap-around dress,' whose finesse was again brought to light by Alaia's drapery-art, is perhaps a notable exception. Kawakubo brings this dialectic to a paradoxical high point. Her dress takes on the character

Figure 5
Comme des Garçons, 1994,
© Steel Stillman.

of stone, in order that the body can become entirely living. The stone folds do not cover the body, in order that it can then be so much the more effectively revealed as marble: they wrap it up warmly, package it. Precisely through this technique, the body underneath the folds is saved from its marble lifelessness, and is granted its freedom and its innocent sensuality again.

The object of this art is an evening gown in the great style. It retains Kawakubo's characteristically aggressive modesty, which for the superficial gaze can be confused with mere raggedness. Perhaps it is only the breaching of the horizon of expectations which conjures up aggression in face of the classical object – one thinks of the Caryatides of Erechtheion. For it seems as if all ideas of craft, be it those of cut or those of symmetry, in short, the very idea of the 'civilized dress,' are affronted by the allusion to the classical model. Not in shimmering, soft silk, but rather, lightly displaced from the luminous marble of the Greek original, the dress stands there in charcoal gray fine-knitted wool-jersey. The complexity of the allusion and its gentle counterfeit is not so easily grasped; it remains below the threshold of attentiveness, as do also the solidity and the unusually artful treatment of the fabric. The dress appears to be made up of two parts, because what one would take to be the undergarment, the tunic, is overlaid with the same material, just as it is the same stone in the case of the statue. Through a completely new technique of draping the cloth on the body, through an invisible stitching and folding, gravity is outwitted, and the fabric is held at the same place at which it would remain on the statue.

The whole effect depends on a fully unsuspected artificiality. Where in antiquity high art was demonstrated by the ability to create the effect of textiles in marble and stone, here the quality of the work is shown in the textile imitation of stone. The result is that one can dance rock'n'roll or, if one wishes, practice karate, in the antique folds. The tunic falls in less pronounced vertical folds, due to the horizontal arrangement of the drapery around the torso – once again a paradoxical exchange of roles with the resistance of stone. Entirely in keeping with the Arcadian idylls of the antique models, it would be frivolous here to speak of a skirt length; the seams are constructed asymmetrically, and can end under the knee or over the ankle, according to the way the dress is worn. The principle of the seam is taken up again in the collar, which is also asymmetrical, triangular and pointed in front, right-angled at the back. The theme of the statue, bringing back into view the norms of antiquity, is exemplary and revealing for the self-conception of a fashion which has its own normative figure in the tailor's dummy. In this creation, the poetics of Rei Kawakubo come to expression.

Through the fusing of various antique models, antiquity is remodeled. The cut of the arm is classic; the cloth is held together over the shoulder, as with a clasp; the strong emphasis of the line that runs under the bottom, and closes off the torso underneath, is characteristic for a certain kind of Aphrodite, the *Anadyomene*, as it is called by archaeologists, whose naked upper body rises out of the folds of a cloth. Here the cloth is wrapped around the hips and knotted to a rise over the sex. The torso in Kawakubo is *ex negativo* emphasized, in that it is not naked, but rather thickly packaged in. As earlier, paradox is here the dominant rhetorical figure. The Aphrodite influence is crossed with another type of antique statue, that of the priestess of Ceres. Its main characteristics are the doubled cloth, *himation*, the horizontal fold of the fabric over the torso, the vertical folding below and finally the poised leg, the knee that presses forth from under the fabric.

The result is marked by the dynamic spiral of an upwards movement. The torso, which, as bearer of the secondary sexual characteristics, is tied and laced up in Western fashion, in order that it can then show forth indirectly under the fabric – firmly formed by a corset or a bra, divided into breast and bottom – appears in Kawakubo's work as a whole torso, as a body. The dressed body summons up the naked body as its counter-image. The torso is not exposed, but rather wrapped in the antique folds, which, by their coloring, remain stone-like without being marmoreal. In the overlays of the stone-like folds, the one thing that the statue definitively excludes, namely that the garments could lose their petrification, becomes possible again: in the textile state, the unjustified anxiety that the covering could fall is left eternally suspended as a possibility. The antique statue is a body again; it has been given back the faculty of movement.

8

Yohji Yamamoto: The Secret Sewn in

It seems to be Yamamoto's fate to be compared to Kawakubo. In many respects, the comparison suggests itself. Both are masters of the multilayered look and of asymmetry; both work primarily in dull colors – in black or in a deep blue; both use red as a light-value rather than as a color, as an equivalent to black; both were responsible for the launching of the *faux vieux* look, the already-used look; both inscribe the history of European fashion into their work. The last point is decisive, not only for what differentiates them from old-world fashion, but also for their treatment of history, for their transformation of fashion into a medium of history. In neither case is this a variation of European historicism, as in Westwood, nor is it a post-modernism, as was too rapidly concluded in some quarters. Postfashion remains modern. It draws post-modern elements back into the project of the moderns, and the Japanese have been the only ones able to do this without falling into a nostalgia for the familiar and the known. If Miyake, in his best works, is the strangest, and Kawakubo, in her best works, is the most modern, so Yamamoto seems the nearest, the most familiar. But as the altogether strange in Miyake tends, in its folding-trickery, towards the native sense for folklore, and the transgressive motifs of Comme des Garçons give expression to an almost forgotten modernity that has now become alien to itself, so also in Yamamoto the proximity comes from further away than romanticizing admirers such as Wim Wenders would like to think.

'My dream is to draw time,' Yamamoto says in Wenders' film, and later: 'The person who works is always beautiful.' While Kawakubo projects a negative aesthetic that draws on aspects of Western modernism for its inspiration, Yamamoto's clothing seems rather to be based on a poetics of memory that has remained untouched by the shocks and traumas of the modern period. The appearance is deceptive, since Yamamoto has expressly placed his work in relation to the war and to Japan's defeat. Nonetheless the dramatic gestures and the pathos that the Western world associates with the negotiation of trauma are altogether absent from Yamamoto's fashion. His work mutely collects and registers the affective traces which make up the individual. The traces of time are, for Yamamoto, traces of destruction, of aging, of decline and of use: traces of death, beautiful because they are ugly. What is important is not the eternal and uniform result of history, but the individualized sum of experiences which are collected in its course. It is the vast field of individual experiences that stands behind his multilayered look. For him, the ideal look is that of 'the vagabonds, the gypsies, the travelers, those who carry their life on their back, everything that they possess, their memories, their treasures, their secrets. This is the perfect dress: one would never be able to create something like that.' Perfection and the supposed progress of history are, for Yamamoto, only the inhuman forms of a flight from this kind of beauty. Beauty lies in what is hidden: it is the secret of the contingent traces, of their collection and their appropriation.

Yamamoto's collections consist in a repertory of forms that is varied from year to year. The basic forms are classical, though Western forms, too, enter into the repertory, *via* a process of creative alienation. The classical double-breasted suit, for example, which is asymmetrically cut out, *mine de rien*. The cut in the back is not centered, one coat-tail is longer than the other. Yamamoto distances and displaces his clothing through slight divergences from expectations. Where Gaultier's revivals operate primarily on the semantic level, through the confrontation of incompatible connotations, Yamamoto's interventions are fashion-immanent, without social index. The impression of an idyllic art of citation originates through a rigorous logic of the forms, without additional moral or social significations. In the winter of 1991/2, for example, the *drag queen*, with clothes made of soft, wafer-thin wool-jersey, trimmed with fine, velvet-like artificial fur, and twined around with luxurious velvet stoles in the same material, diffuses a confused sexiness, very much related to the historical models from the time of Shakespeare; the impression is completed by stockings, again in the same material, which reach their end halfway up the thigh. The combination of fur and fabric, whose differing weights are exploited for the modeling of the outfit, displaces the exhibition of sexual characteristics characteristic of the genre of the drag-queen outfit on to the surface of the material, de-centering and disseminating the sexual motif through the configuration of the weave. The sex remains, unusually, shyly hidden. Yamamoto hides the open secret of transvestism – which does not mean that he denies it. Or again, the *bag lady*, in a very crumpled suit, interwoven with silver threads, no doubt her Sunday dress, which looks from a distance as if it were the strikingly elegant suit of a manager. Here the irony of the concealment is clearer, and can be linked to a critical semantics. But the secret of its charm is untouched by the moral, that it steals away from us.

The technical distinction of Yamamoto's fashion stems from researches into the relation of body and garment, and from a remarkable feeling for space. Kawakubo's statues invoke a similar understanding of space in antiquity. Many of the most elaborate creations of Yamamoto can be seen as scientific experiments. In their refinement and labor-intensiveness, they are easily the equal of the old *haute couture*. Later the results attained in these very complicated constructions are almost invisibly worked into apparently simpler creations – for example, the red dress from the spring and summer collection of 1992 (Figure 6).

If one follows up the experiments of Yamamoto or Kawakubo, sooner or later one is led to Madeleine Vionnet, whose cutting technique created a body that was no longer divided into a two-dimensional plane, composed of a front and a back side, but rather self-moving and three-dimensional, its form constantly changing in space. The fabric modeled the body in different ways,

Figure 6
Yohji Yamamoto, 1992,
© Yohji Yamamoto, Tokyo
1988–9.

depending on whether it was cut with, against or diagonal to the weave of the thread; only in this way did the fabric allow its weight and its elasticity to be modified. This technique was used by Vionnet for mimetic purposes, i.e. for idealizing exaggeration. The flow of the movements was underlined, the lines of the body were made softer. According to the then prevailing ideology of fashion, all individual weaknesses had to be compensated for, in the interest of an ideal body-image. Behind Vionnet's clothes stood the femininity of the classical statue. Garments flowing flatteringly all around it; the statue-woman embodied an ideal. Yamamoto appropriates Vionnet's technique for his own purposes – not in order to establish a normativized beauty in a static space, but rather to reveal the beauty of the incomplete and the imperfect: a transitory beauty, beauty in transit.

Yamamoto's red dress is made from a strangely unpretentious silk-crêpe, lightly transparent but also completely matt, which brings out the quality of the red. The cloth doubles the body, and lightly staggers its movements. Instead of being harmonized into one movement by the flow of the lines, the space of an interval is introduced in between three-dimensional dress-body and the body. To this purpose, Yamamoto cut the material such that the fields of force of the individual lengths of material reciprocally block each other, like vectors which do not accumulate down-wards in a sweeping fall of the fabric, but rather collide obliquely and repel one another. Cut out round in the front, and pointed at the back, the fabric is wide around the shoulders, and falls down to the middle of the calf. It is simply pulled on, without buttons or zips, like an undergarment – this too, a reference to Vionnet, who introduced lingerie techniques and ceased to line her dresses, so that they would hug the body better. Here this technique is applied to quite different ends. In the age of stretch-fabrics, the stitching is given a new function. As it lets the dress fit to the body, it dynamizes the fields of force within the material, causing patterns to originate at the surface.

The red dress, as casual as it seems – the publicity photo showed a black girl playing basketball under a highway – is in fact as labor-intensive as the *haute couture*. Since it is composed from at least twenty different pieces of material, it has to be individually cut out. Where a good part of the art of *haute couture* consists in making the dart of the fabric disappear, it is here not only left visible, but made into an arabesque ornament. What is sewed in is turned outward for decoration. The dart, the line at which the fabric is doubled, shimmers through the thin material like a pattern. The staging of the dress is similarly paradoxical: worn with sneakers and cycling gloves, it proposes itself as sportswear, precisely that which brought the *haute couture* to its end.

Despite the apparent potential of sport to let everyone look the same, and thus to compensate for the normativizing thrust of fashion, the effect of the sportswear and recreation industries has been precisely the opposite. Yamamoto's tailor-made red dress, on the other hand, really does do away with the invisible power of the norm. No two copies are identical: even trying it on is only of limited help, since the dress that one tries was cut out for another woman, and bears her form. The red dress inconspicuously preserves the secret of the individual, transforming the supposed flaws of individual divergence from a supposed ideal norm into the beauty of an arabesque. Breaking with the ideal of the *haute couture*, Yamamoto does not wish to pour the individual into the most flattering possible form; but nor does he simply leave the individual to be what it was. The individual here becomes the finest ornament of all, and is to be worn; it becomes the shape of *haute couture* after sportswear. If the normativization of the individual to an ideal form is here abandoned, this does not imply a realism or a factualism, beyond all norms: rather, through the dress, a secret idealization of individual traces of divergence is effected.

That which, in the red dress, is literally sewn in and almost made to disappear, is splendidly turned outwards in the evening gown. In Figure 7, the dress from the winter collection of 1989/90 is made out of a heavy, glossy triacetate which stands even more heavily than taffeta. Overlapping 'cloth bags' are sewn onto the corset that supports it, opening upwards on the top and downwards on the skirt, and folding over one another in a confusing disorder at the arms and around the *decolleté*. The bodice is closed at the back with a zip, which is concealed by folds with press studs. Such an obviously handmade display of splendor is altogether *haute couture*, an outbidding of *prêt-à-porter*.

The anti-mimetic basis of this sculpture does not lie in the display of feminine forms in artificial isolation in the manner of the nineteenth century. Rather it is a matter of a sublime en-cryptation, a form of sublimation which, once again, consists in the inconspicuous and indefinable distance created between dress and body. One does not see, cannot even guess, where the dress lies on the body. As with many of Miyake's creations, the work has something of the paper-folding effect of origami.

The *decolleté* is surrounded by asymmetrical folds, which pass over into the arms. On top of the actual body, perceptible only at the waist, a voluminous second body is stretched, like a flower – a very abstract flower, certainly, in which geometric forms have replaced organic forms. The promise of this bloom, the body which will come forth when it loses its petals, and for which the flower is a metaphor, is a complicated nothingness. Under

Figure 7
Yohji Yamamoto, 1989–90,
© Yohji Yamamoto, Tokyo
1988–9.

these abstractions, it has dissolved itself into air; neck and head, emerging from the splendor of the dress like a calyx, belong to an elfin astral body which, scarcely to be guessed at in the midst of this sculpture, has its place in the midst of nowhere.

Yamamoto's most experimental and demanding creation has affinities with an old and a new schema of clothing: knight's armor and machine-man. A three-piece trouser suit, consisting of a black T-shirt with a small stand-up collar in wool-jersey, trousers in black wool-felt and a kind of show-cuirass, a shirt of mail consisting of a wool-felt in the back part and a complicated (though unpainted) plywood creation at the front (Figure 8). On both sides of the trousers, plywood pieces are attached by massive thumbscrews, marking the position of the ankle: these correspond to the calf and the thigh, and recall the ballet drawings of Oskar Schlemmer. The pure light wood which, in its fully unprocessed state, is more delicate than any silk, invokes the atelier, the project-character of the piece.

On the sleeves and the collar of the T-shirt, wood panels are set together with fine hinges and screws, a detail in which one sees the meticulous hand of the designer. They make the

Figure 8
Yohji Yamamoto, 1992, ©
Yohji Yamamoto, Tokyo.

metallic, glossy crudeness of old or new armor ridiculous. The mail shirt, put together out of more than twenty separate pieces, oscillates between the unwieldiness of the models it evokes and the tenderness of the execution. It stands slightly apart from the body at the front, and has to be adjusted with the aid of a felt ribbon at the back. Certain restrictions on one's movement notwithstanding, the whole piece is light and almost comfortable to wear. The space between the garment and body makes it easier that it looks. The result is a silhouette which adds a foreign volume to the body which, for its part, almost disappears, wrapped up in the elegant, black, soft, warm dress.

In the epoch that the garment cites, the body was supposed to fill out the form. Here, however, it has withdrawn itself. Comfortably packed into wool-jersey, it stands, like a crab or a turtle, inside a framework with which it does not form a whole. The moveability of the fabric stands in sharp contrast to the brittleness of the wood; the coarseness of the trousers contrasts with the finely articulated woodwork of the jacket. The half-round, moon-like wooden coat-tails mounted onto the jacket cite the cuirass of a Spanish military commander, and make for a formal transition to the more roundly cut pieces attached to the trousers. The mimetic moment created by the way the trousers follow the movement of the legs is completely lost from the jacket, in the interest of the intricate technique that is necessary if one wants to make clothes from plywood. Putting these clothes on requires a certain ceremonial, reminiscent of the dressing ceremonies of the seventeenth century; the complexities of the nineteenth century corset demanded a similar input of time and assistance. Screws are used as buttons, and one has to have a chambermaid, or other help, in order to get into the mail-shirt. The splendor of this work would be entirely equal to that of the great court costumes of the sixteenth and seventeenth centuries, if it were not for the absence of every brilliance in the colors, and the decidedly trivial materials. Black felt and black wool-jersey disappear, without luster: the wood is rough, neither lacquered nor painted, not even ornamented or polished.

Freed from all masculine warlike associations, the utterly simple, untreated material reveals itself as the purest possible feminine adornment. In the background stands the play with the metaphor of armor: an affinity is suggested between the corset, the classic feminine armor, and the knight's armor. The corset, whose whalebone ribs provided a hard external support where the inner structure of the skeleton had failed to perform, is here turned outwards in an almost grotesque way. It no longer has the everyday supportive function, nor that of martial defense. The construction of the skeleton seems to be imposed on the wearer from outside. But she is the one who wears it, and she wears it alone, as adornment, and for fun.

9

Gaultier: Revaluation of All Values

With the unerring step of a sleepwalker, Jean-Paul Gaultier's work goes ever again straight to the concept of taste itself. In questioning taste, he strikes at the very heart of the century of fashion. According to the criteria of the taste that has been lovingly cultivated over centuries, his fashion is completely tasteless. His ongoing deconstruction of Paris fashion is a kind of surrealism against the grain, which consciously makes a fool of itself. From the historical point of view, his work mobilizes Schiaperelli, the fashion designer of the surrealists, against Chanel, the designer of the classic, comfortable understatement. Schiaperelli's is an art of the surprising, absurd detail, which focuses attention on the dress; the contrast could not be greater with Chanel, a fashion which erases itself, which consciously does *not* present itself as art, applying its whole skill, on the contrary, to make the dress disappear behind the mask of the personality.

Chanel grafted the understatement of the English landed gentry, with its not so frequently washed wool, tweed and jersey, onto the fashion of the French court aristocracy, devoted to representation and splendor. The fashion equivalent of the total artwork, as presented by Poiret, with its baroque display of splendor, is an image of the festivities of the court. Schiaparelli carried this over into exaggerated avant-garde nonsense. Entirely in this 'courtly' tradition, Gaultier is one of the first to make a fashion for men which is no less striking and extravagant than women's fashion. With his work, the nineteenth-century male renunciation has definitively come to an end. Just like women, his men wear artificial fur, lurid colors, conspicuous cuts, skintight leggings. Even the codpiece has been resurrected to display the family jewels in their old European splendor.

Gaultier's clothing pushes itself into the foreground, springs to the eye. Here, in the place of the representational finery of the court, in the place of avant-garde artistic aspirations, there is a childish delight in disguise. But this delight has lost its innocence, and lets the megalomania of the petit bourgeois have free rein: *toc*, kitsch, flashiness and shameless showing off, in all its gruesome beauty, step in for art, and finery. The discreet charm of the bourgeoisie is over and done with. Absolute taboos of good taste – of that taste which resided in large part in the sublimation of physicality, its replacement by an artistic textile body – are broken by obscene allusions. A *decolleté* is decorated with black, stringy strands of wool, instead of feathers, evoking fashion's strictest taboo: body hair.

The play of disguise in Gaultier has nothing to do with historical idylls, with the evocation of a place outside of time, nothing to do with Sleeping Beauty Romanticism or the fragrant lost paradises of 'childhood loves'; nor is it related to the redeemed temporality of art, the patina of history, and the kind of beauty that comes with this. In Gaultier, rather, this play carries a precise social and historical index – including the announcement of its own obsolescence. His fashion does not distill a timeless value or essence, cleansed of the traces of time, and with it, of all triviality and contingency. On the contrary, it even reduces that which had been the specifically 'fashionable' element, that in which lay the specific attractiveness of fashion – the temptation of the moment. Instead, Gaultier instructs us again in the joy of flaunting, here isolated in its pure form, through the artificial exhibition of sexedness. All the citations from the history of costume, of which Gaultier makes a more abundant use than any designer before him, ultimately point to this one signification. The archaeology of the history of costume – and Gaultier's fashion is nothing if not this – discovers its origins in the perpetual sexual bravado and exhibitionism of both sexes. The electric blue or green of the feathers decorating a *decolleté* of Poiret, the brilliant red plastic nails twisted together to make a scarf, *à la* Schiaparelli, the Spanish grandee, the shirt-dress of Balenciaga, the Napoleonic officer, the Miami beach-girl, the wet-look-leather girl of the 1960s, the exotic floral swinging skirt, the Siberian officer's coat – all of this is nothing but boasting, a display of sexual glory.

Gaultier's clothes expose this boasting-effect as such. But the wearer who is permitted to experience the pleasures of showing off is nonetheless required to maintain a certain distance. The act of flaunting itself is thematized, and this thematization is also worn, when one wear the clothes. Gaultier's fashion is all about distance – not about authenticity or identity. As in Yamamoto, but for other reasons, the drag queen is the most attractive example. She is not what she pretends to be, but she enjoys a specific pleasure in the play of deceptive similarity. With all its openly exhibited perversity, Gaultier's fashion, in its peculiar ugliness, retains something childish and crude; at one moment the effect is surprising, at the next it is comic. All who have had the good fortune to experience Gaultier's annual sale in the rue Vivienne will recall the impression of an astonishing imaginative productivity. Just as children untiringly try out the possible variations of what they find in the grandparents' attic, so Gaultier has plundered the attic of fashion, and offers his customers his most daring and cheeky finds. Not infrequently, he discovers a wholly new cut, just in order to distance the citation of a certain period; no effort is too great to achieve a new effect of disguise, and this always for its own sake alone. The *enfant terrible* of the French fashion world refuses only one possibility: the dutiful *chic* of respectable people, *bon chic, bon genre, bcbg.*

Gaultier made clear his attitude towards that which is designated *bon chic bon genre* on the occasion of the ambitious exhibition *Le monde selon ses créateurs*. The horizon of expectations for the overall in Figure 9 is formed by the classic men's double-breasted suit, with silver buttons, a rather loose cut, trousers falling in soft folds, turned up at the ankles: a moment of men's fashion from the 1940s, *à la* Humphrey Bogart. On the breast pocket there is an embroidered emblem, an honorary insignia perhaps, concealed in the manner of the dandy, by a

Figure 9

Jean-Paul Gaultier, 1991, in
Le monde et ses créateurs,
Jean-Paul Gaultier, Romeo
Gigli, Vivienne Westwood,
Sybilla, Martin Margiela,
Jean-Charles Castelbajac,
Musée de la Mode et du
Costume, Palais Galliera.

beige, black-spotted handkerchief. As the suit flips over into the overall, so the emblem of social standing turns into the sign of a specific garage or workshop. The midsection is irresistibly comic; all the while preserving the traditional cut in pedantically exact detail, pockets included, the jacket suddenly proceeds on to the pants, without interruption. The two-piece becomes a one-piece, recalling the unbroken outline of a comic figure silhouette. The virtuosic accomplishment of the cut succeeds where the sociologists have failed: bourgeois white-collar and proletarian blue-collar enter into an alliance of fashion. The success of the piece shows up a secret masculine complicity between the chauffeur and the chauffeured, in the conflict of the connotations and in the difference in the instinctual vicissitudes. Gaultier's motto: 'Je participe à la confusion totale des valeurs.' Two mutually exclusive forms of sexuality encounter each other, with a knowing wink of the eyes. Where the conventional suit, with its jacket as a little coat of honor, announces the erotics of power, although at the cost of physicality, the overall stands for the physical potency of the working man. The overall is, for more than one reason, a practical people's garment, not least because, as the quotidian myth has it, the man is almost naked underneath.

The small, would-be great man of the people, in Gaultier's self-presentation, is not unaccompanied. The blazer of his companion shown in Figure 10 is as perfect and as blue as one could possibly

Figure 10
Jean-Paul Gaultier, 1991, in
Le monde et ses créateurs,
Jean-Paul Gaultier, Romeo
Gigli, Vivienne Westwood,
Sybilla, Martin Margiela,
Jean-Charles Castelbajac,
Musée de la Mode et du
Costume, Palais Galliera.

imagine: single-breasted, with gold buttons, one naturally expects to see it paired with a whiter than white blouse-collar, in whose freshness the program of *bon genre* would find its fulfillment. Actually, the blouse is absent, but not the suitably beige trousers, in which the sex is suspended in favor of competence, in the classically discreet manner demanded by the genre. As in the men's suit, however, Gaultier de-conventionalizes this most conventional of all solutions.

The white blouse is alienated into the *decolleté* of an evening gown in which the shoulders are left bare, destroying the neutrality of the successful professional woman through the attraction of her idle predecessor. In a paradoxical effect, the nakedness of the shoulders stands forth more strikingly than could ever have been achieved by the suggestion of the former aura. Formally, this is because, in contrast to the evening gown, the nakedness here is the only exposed part in an otherwise strictly closed ensemble, in which even the hands are covered – an ensemble whose *raison d'être* is to neutralize eroticism through mimicry of the male suit. But here the repressed unexpectedly returns, and the erotically charged man at the wheel has met his match.

Paradoxalement sportive – the dress of this name (Figure 11) stems from the collection *femme* of winter 1991/2. It vacillates between evening gown, cocktail dress and associated professional wardrobe. The confusion between day and night, between work and party, is not here a matter of versatility, as in the example of the well-received silk parka combined with cashmere pullover which, with its mix of sportiness and elegance, could be worn anywhere and everywhere. On the contrary, it seems equally inappropriate as evening or as daywear; the type, the role, the function, the age for which the dress is intended is unclear. Not for the society lady, not for the career woman, not for the intellectual, nor for the sweetheart – all the clichés seem to be set aside; and over the whole thing, there is an air of Harlequin and *Commedia dell'arte*. As in the good old times, it has a name that suits the Harlequin: *paradoxalement sportive*.

In the background, although one does not see this unless one takes a second look, stands the kilt – not, however, the Scottish checked skirt which wins praise every year again. The kilt is evoked in the completely new skirt cut which Gaultier showed in various designs for the winter of 1991/2, a cut so decorative and of such amazing simplicity that one had to wonder why no-one had

Figure 11
Jean-Paul Gaultier, 1991–2,
© Steel Stillman.

come up with it before. As so often in dressmaking, the simplicity
of the cut in no way alters the fact that it actually involves an
ingenious geometrical figure. What begins innocuously enough
as a T-shirt cut, falls apart underneath the belt-line in four tails
of great regularity, but with strangely broken rhythm.

This effect is achieved by a cut which involves horizontal
rather than vertical lengths of material, extending out beyond
the silhouette on the right and the left in the same proportions
that they hang down in the front and the back. Laid down flat
there emerges an upside-down T, whose horizontal wings can be
wrapped around the hips and tied behind the back with a button.

But this T is more impressive worn open: under the weight of the lengths that lead right and left, and whose corners fall apart from one another to form regular rectangles, the skirt then hangs down in tails or flaps around the moving body.

A relative solid white-wool-jersey follows the silhouette of the body in the top, then the skirt solidly swings as if it were flared. In this version of the dress, its geometry is emphasized by stiff, black velvet strips; they bring out, paradoxically, both the right and the left leaning widths of the skirt, as well as its shortness on the right and left flanks. Before and behind, these strips accentuate the splendid breadth of the skirt; at the side they mark and weigh down the fall of the lengths of the fabric, and push the material that falls to the side toward the middle. A deep-red stand-up collar, positioned as the horizontal to the black vertical lines, indicates the form of the cut as an emblem of the whole. A hanger loop in white jersey on the velvet strips at the back, Gaultier's profane label, preserves the only-too-perfectly staged creation from suffocating in its own emblematic wealth. Harsh as the determining contrast of black and red on the white background is, the heraldic stridency of the emblem dissolves itself in the falling of the material, and does not allow the stiffness of the costume, fleetingly evoked, to prevail. The modern sport-citation of the hanger loop is symptomatic, an irony-signal referring to the carnivalesque vacillation between uniform-skirt and city-emblem that the piece sets in motion. In spite of all of this, there is a peculiar, unsuspected ceremoniousness to the work. It is as if one could after all go to the ball in sportswear, with flying skirts like never before, and in a splendor undimmed by any process of reduction.

10

Helmut Lang: Fabric, Skin, Figure

The German philosopher Hegel dedicated several pages of his *Aesthetics* to what he viewed as a trivial and thoroughly feminine subject, to wit, the fashions of modern and antique clothing, and, in the process, assured himself of his own masculinity by accusing his fashion-crazed contemporaries of effeminacy. He declared a preference for fully dressed statues and proceeded to praise the advantages of antique vis-à-vis modern dress. 'Our sense of propriety,' he writes, 'shies away from presenting completely nude figures.' He was quick to point out, however, that this custom has its good points, too:

> For, as the dress, instead of covering up a physical position or pose, allows it to shine through completely, so not only is nothing lost, but quite on the contrary, the pose is lifted more fully into view. In this respect, then, clothing would even need to be regarded as an advantage, in so far as it removes from our view the immediate aspect of that which, by being merely sensual, is also meaningless.[1]

Clothing, writes Roland Barthes, encapsulating Hegel's argument, turns mere sensuality into sense, and gives meaning to something that is, as such, quite meaningless – human flesh – by bestowing upon it a shape that adds a spiritual dimension to the purely sensual one.[2]

This sensual–senseless dimension of the body must be concealed as a necessary precondition for the moving silhouette to appear in all its 'intricate, free, and living outline.' For Hegel, modern clothing does not do justice to this requirement. For, although it does trace the outlines of the figure by means of narrow sleeves or tights and trousers showing some leg, those outlines tend, by and large, to lose their 'beautiful organic curves' by being stuck inside 'stretched sacks with hard creases.' In place of an 'organic moulding of the limbs,' instead of 'sensually beautiful roundedness,' we perceive something 'so cut up, and stitched together here, and stretched over there, and stiff everywhere, an altogether unfree assemblage of shapes and folds and areas, squeezed this way and that according to the requirements of seams, buttonholes, and buttons.' In short: 'The sensual aspect of a mechanically worked-over piece of fabric.'[3]

Hegel, then, was less than euphoric about modern clothing which, he claimed, 'merely wrecks the shapes of the limbs' on account of its being 'pulled this way and that' by its seams; even where it may be permitted a free flow of folds, it is subjected not to the will of the natural–organic but to the willfulness of the couturier and the wiles of fashion. Anne Hollander, in contrast, views the modern male suit (which took its first tentative steps into the world in Hegel's time) as accomplishing precisely what Hegel regards as the sole prerogative of antique habiliments. The suit, says Hollander, makes an antique hero of any man, an ideal, sexually potent, naked figure underneath naturally pliable wool, linen and leather. Thanks to the modern couturier's art, any man might acquire the handsome proportions of an antique statue cast in bronze or marble.

To Hollander, then, the modern suit is not a piece of clothing that forces the body into creased disfigurement by the dictates of its own poor craftsmanship. She views it, rather, as an 'attractive disguise of nudity.' That she considers this to be sexy may be a tribute to the *Zeitgeist*, which will describe anything it finds pleasing as sexy, even where its sexiness may have been dispersed into complete abstraction.[4]

For all their variant estimates of modern clothing, Hegel and Hollander share an antipathy to the merely fashionable, and they also share the claim that clothes should effect an idealization through sublimation – a sublimation, that is, of the body, etherealized and absolved of almost all those inherently meaningless fleshly qualities. Only in such a way is the body made naturally beautiful. Ideal expression requires sublimation as its precondition. For the human figure to appear in its authentic– natural and sexually potent form (in Hollander's version) or in its spiritual–organic and naturally beautiful incarnation (as Hegel would have it) the material element must be made to disappear. On the one hand, the mere flesh, the bare skin, the insignificant nakedness, has to go, while, on the other, the materiality of the fashioning should vanish. The claim that naturalness may be constructed by means of a perfect cut of the fabric follows from Hegel's statements almost as a natural conclusion – he is, after all, in this chapter talking about sculpture. It is Hollander, on the other hand, who points out that the new natural–authentic, ideal body-shape has to be the product of an ever more refined and intricate cutting technique. It is only through the art of couture that the classic true-to-nature human shape can be realized. The human being's ideal nakedness is achieved at a price – that of being dressed.

With so much enthusiasm floating about for the ideals of antiquity it seems almost redundant to point out that what we are dealing with here is a classicistic concept of beauty. This is the basis of all modern fashion, and has remained the endur- ing guiding light of all designers up to the present day, who avowedly do not sell fashion, but offer only natural elegance, plain authenticity, clearly-cut purist simplicity and complete understatement, so that one may feel comfortably at ease and at home within one's own perfectly sublimated body, and become coolly and unmistakably at one with oneself.

Until the classicist period, fashion had not concerned itself with the aim of emphasizing the organic naturalness of the body's limbs and proportions, nor had it bothered tracing it mimetically and thus presenting its form and content up to critical appreciation. Instead, fashion used the body as carrier of a quite different silhouette, imposing upon it another shape altogether, not in order to make it appear more natural but in order to make it more imposing and more capable of commanding respect. Reminders of such variant fashion ideals may be seen in the extremely elongated shapes current in the Gothic period, the armour-like, very flat, upper-body vestments seen at the Elizabethan court, hoop-skirts, crinolines, or the short, puffily-upholstered pants worn by sixteenth century male nobility. Such body impositions also celebrated a brief, glamorous comeback during the New Look of the 1950s.

This obviously non-natural remodeling of the body by means of clothes and the invention of another silhouette incorporating the body as carrier, has not altogether disappeared from the field of fashion. Today's fashion does, however, remain solidly rooted within a reference back to the modern, classicistic standard. Perhaps the most sophisticated practitioners of this dual mode are designers like Miyake, Comme des Garçons or Yamamoto. On the one hand, these Japanese designers can draw on a dizzying repertoire of historic forms and shapes in which the relationship between body and dress is determined quite differently than in the European tradition; on the other hand, they have a radically defamiliarized perspective on European shapes and impositions upon the human figure. Not content merely to parody and sally forth with hyperbole, as Westwood does, they like to disfigure their designs. Kawakubo's Angel Collection (from the summer of 1997) develops the most breathtaking aesthetic effects on the basis of such disfigurations.

Other designers deconstruct the classicistic ideal. Margiela's collections specifically spotlight those skills and tricks of the artisan that help to produce the etherealized natural body. Margiela's most fascinating designs seem to be accompanied by a fast-forward version of the history of the couturier's craft and trade, and they direct the viewer's attention to that which, in Hegel's opinion, could only have been to the detriment of any organic beauty: to the materials and their workmanship, to the art of *couture*.

Lang utilizes the historical repertory of superimpositional forms for neither parody nor for deconstruction, but for a diffusion and dissolution of the classic/natural figure and its 'organic roundednesses and curves.' His research has concentrated not merely on cutting techniques but also on materials. His collections present a baffling array of unusual and novel materials, especially from the realm of plastics, including new types of volume, different ways of falling, and new sorts of gleaming, and activate the haptic sense in hitherto unknown ways. The question remains in precisely which way these things are connected – the diffuse and flittering silhouette and the purely sensual, the as-and-by-itself-insignificant, the naked skin, the bare flesh? The question brings us to the domain of female fashion, where the interplay between veiling and unveiling, and the partial exposure of the body is a constitutive quality. The male body remains, classically, fully covered; uncovered, it is at best, sporty, at worst, ridiculous. It is never erotically invested. The contrast between bare skin and fabric material dominates the matrix of feminine fashion.

Eroticism, Barthes has written, is another word for that brief moment when skin flashes out from behind the cloth. The erotic quality of that instant lies in its transgression of a codification. The early Barthes, still wholly structuralist and reductive, understood fashion in this way, where even nakedness signifies a kind of being dressed.[5] The framed nakedness – that strip of skin on the upper arm between a long glove and a sleeveless dress – is contrasted against the unexpected, unintentional, intimate instant in which skin is seen flashing up between two strips of fabric; in other words, a nakedness that does not signify a state of being dressed, just nakedness that seems sensually insignificant. But even this form of nakedness has been encoded since the eighteenth century within the shape of the negligé, and rests upon paired contrasts like premeditated/public versus unintentional/private. It, too, is based upon a precondition of a shaped, contained body and a silhouette, and a clear relationship between the whole and its parts. The instant is erotic precisely because it does not merely flash up a glimpse of sensually insignificant naked flesh, but because it shows framed naked skin that is recognizably an erotically marked part of a whole figure. The merely sensual, the naked flesh, tends to engender rather more horror than lust. It is less a taboo than a limiting value of fashion which, in the final analysis, rests upon its sublimation or fetishization.

Fashion appears to have acquired some support in this transformation process, where the mere flesh, that which is purely sensual and hence senselessly naked, can be laden with meaning and become eroticized. The codification of the body has long since, and with equal rights for both sexes, moved below the skin. The flesh is shaped through exercise much more rigorously than in the past through the corset, and marked with injections, incisions, intrusions and inscriptions of signs, through bodybuilding, piercing, tattooing and branding. Lang's work circles around this context of merely insignificant sensuality and its codification.

It is no accident that Holzer and Lang's project for the Florence Biennale Art/Fashion 1996 should have been based on a contrasting treatment of the joint themes of dress and skin. In Holzer's segment, entitled 'I can smell you on my skin, I can smell you on my clothes,' the impurities of a skin type that does not conform to the accepted ideals of beauty are presented up to the viewer in stark close-ups devoid of any high-flown ideals. Here, a powerfully uneven skin texture is displayed warts and all, its unbearable flesh-color tones heightened by pigment disturbances and small blood vessels visible under the skin – an effect as intimate and non-ideal as the smell which may well issue from such skin. In a move reminiscent of Süskind's *Perfume*, Holzer and Lang also insisted on getting the smell of humanity distilled – the smell of not quite freshly-washed skin and of clothes worn a number of days in a row – and then having this smell sprayed into the rooms of the exhibition. Lang contrasts codified skin with mere skin.

His photo-diptychs take as their twin themes the martyrdom of Christ and the difference between the genders. The first diptych shows a man wearing a T-shirt depicting a woodcut-like print of the head of Christ, with the crown of thorns; at the same time, the man himself bears a certain semblance to the saviour with the tragically beautiful features traced on the sweat-cloth of Veronica. The opposite side displays the inner sanctum of a classicist church, whose overpowering elegance appears to be hurtling towards a single vanishing point, the cross on the side altar. Never has flesh seemed more replete with significance. The second diptych shows two portraits. On the one side is a head-and-shoulders photograph of a very frail and fragile-looking boy (Figure 12) whose beauty has nothing in common with the ideals of classic antiquity or the physical transformations achieved in modern-day bodybuilding. He displays Beardsleyesque tattoos on the theme of Wilde's *Salomé*, the tender branding-scars on his arms, his braided plaits and a uniform cap with gleaming laquered bill pushed down over his eyes. On the opposite side, one perceives what I believe may still be referred to as a beautiful woman (Figure 13). In what is perhaps the final version

Figure 12
Helmut Lang, 1997, in
Art/Fashion, Guggenheim
Museum SoHo, New York.

of Blind Cupid with Venus, her sceptical glance contrasts with
his unseeing gaze, just as his exposed nipples contrast with her
covered ones in a metonymic juxtaposition to the eyes. What
might appear at first glance to be a representational portrait
of a lady in a strapless evening gown is quickly revealed as an
intimate photograph when it becomes clear that the woman has
in fact merely dropped her jacket from her shoulders and that
her *décolleté* is framed by underwear in the shape of a white
brassiere with dangling straps. The naked skin of the exposed
shoulders and *décolleté* might represent codification in its purest
sense were it not for the underwear. Precisely because this is
neither specifically erotic nor seductively intimate, it causes the
body suddenly to appear in a state of naked undress.

Lang presents a counter-program to Holzer's. Holzer shows
bare flesh with superimposed lettering in contrasting tones of flesh
and varying degrees of magnification. Lang, on the other hand,
displays eroticism as a clash of different horizons of expectation
resulting from the invocation and transgression of codes. Hence,
while bare flesh may be turned into a subject matter of art and

Figure 13
Helmut Lang, 1999, in
*Louise Bourgeois. Jenny
Holzer. Helmut Lang*,
Kunsthalle Wien.

can even be projected to the point of gagging disgust, in fashion
it must retain the fascination of a limiting calculus; ideally, it
requires transformation into eroticism. Fashion is a commentary
upon garments that is expressed in other garments – an ever-
new and unique distortion of the codes erected in the shape of
garments. Therein lies its enduring fascination.

Perhaps it is no more than coincidence, but, if so, a fortunate
one, that Lang's breakthrough has been repeatedly linked to a
certain red, narrowly-cut rubber dress with black lace applica-
tions. Its special gimmick lay not in the oft-cited talcum powder
that one had to dust oneself in before getting into it, nor in its
squeakiness, nor even in the intrusion of fetishist paraphernalia
into the domain of fashion, but rather in its paradoxical combination of opaque latex and transparent lace. Latex is to S/M-
fashion what furs were to Sacher-Masoch. Latex encases the body
within a tight fit, imprisoning it both elastically and firmly while
echoing each and every one of its movements through a second
layer of skin. Hyper-naked, the body is thus simultaneously
severely constrained and impossible to touch. It is a well-known

fact that latex cannot be shed or rolled out of with any degree of ease. Lace is the counter-program. It reveals touchable skin and transforms the body from an over-precise silhouette into an arabesque. Lace placed upon latex is like Klimt superimposed on Sacher-Masoch, all within the same Vienna.

In this anti-idealistic manner, Lang's fashion has continued to dissolve the clear outline of the body's silhouette, and to further confuse it through the defamiliarizing superimposition of various historical modes of shaping the body through clothing. Such layerings of materials and silhouettes do not expose the underlying figure so much as they permit it to appear as one among several possible silhouettes that blend into one another without giving privilege to any one clearly defined figure or shape. This effect is heightened by the volume and transparency of the materials employed, such as a porous polyester with an appearance of pleated three-dimensionality, shot through at irregular intervals with more translucent portions. The fragments of naked skin visible through the irregularities of the material are not particularly erotically marked, but depend for their effect entirely on the coincidental interplay of irregularities in the fabric and of the body as it becomes visible, as if by chance, underneath the material. Conventional expectations are, as a matter of principle, displaced rather than fulfilled. Thus, a skirt may be reminiscent of a tennis frock while its white pleats may fail to respond to movement, even the least little bit, insisting instead on stiffly and firmly staying in place. Or a wafty, thinly pleated skirt may not succeed in hiding the undergarment that gives it its shape; indeed, it would appear that the skirt had been especially designed in such a fashion as to allow the undergarment to shine through with particular boldness and, at the same time, impenetrability.

The relationship between skin, fabric and body shape is shown in an exemplary manner by a dress from the winter collection of 1997/8. It consists entirely of gleaming black or silvery-grey ribbons of satin stitched together so as to leave open spaces and produce garlands of a kind found in any haberdashery shop. Where these adhere closely to the body, they present an impenetrable gleaming surface, but in all other places through which the skin, depending on the body's movements, can be glimpsed, they open up into swirling vents. The silhouette dissolves as these garlands, producing effects of light and shadow on the skin, render the dress almost three-dimensional. It seems to suggest yet another body over and above the one more hidden than shown below, one whose main effect, being dependent upon the lower body's every movement, lies in revealing a lozenge-shaped oval of that body in its naked state. Here, again, skin is seen at the price of figure. The nakedness revealing itself follows chance movements and cannot be pre-arranged. By contrast, one can think of Versace, where every baring of skin is carefully framed and sexiness is set into action in a manner as dramatical as it is predictable.

In this context, the use of satin in the form of artificial satin ribbons, has a double twist. On the one hand, in an ironic, self-referential touch, the sartorial trade itself is referenced. At the same time, however, the traditional function of satin is radically subverted. Silk, so gleaming, smooth, cosseting and flowing, caresses and embraces the body with its myriad of shimmering mirror-lights, shapes and moulds it softly, especially if the material is cut sideways, at an angle to the thread, in accordance with the cutting principles perfected by Vionnet. Satin is the material with the most attractive flow and fall. In the case of this dress, the ribbons of satin also fall, though in a quite different way. Rippling over the body's surface instead of clinging to it, the satin ribbons slide apart and twist themselves into an a-mimetic play of light and shadow. In spite of its inimitable fall, then, satin cannot function as a second skin here; instead, it shows by chance whatever naked skin should happen to become visible.

In the summer collection of 1998, this dress of ribbons arrived in another version, in which, in place of the impenetrable satin, diaphanous polyester ribbons – of a very light blue, for example – were used. Here, what became visible underneath its readily opening garlands, loosely flowing around the body, was an equally light blue dress of an almost over-simplistic ribbed silk evocative of men's underthings. As comfortably flattering as it is to wear, it does little to capture the voyeur's attention because the relationship between outer garment and undergarment seems, in this case, to have been reversed. The flimsy transparent outer dress reveals an item of underclothing beneath that is impenetrable to the eye and that with its heavier ribbed material conveys an impression of almost sporty robustness.

Another version of the second skin theme is played through on a shin-length dress from the winter collection 1997/8 in gleaming blood-red silk of hyper-thin translucence – a cross between S/M and an antique statue. The silk, appearing here about as valuable as trash, gives the impression of having been designed, by the addition of a pinch of Elasteen, for the specific purpose of following the curvature of the body through its every movement. Below the bosom, the torso is cut apart by traces of seams. Although one seam runs along beneath the chest, this does not give an impression of Empire, but a slightly pinched appearance of the breast akin to that of a shirt worn a tad too tight. From a distance, the seams are reminiscent of antique pleating, although on this occasion they do not produce a spiritually heightened, clear silhouette, but form only small bags of bunched material, disfiguring the shape of the body. In contrast to the S/M scenarios of bondage the seams evoke, they do not serve as sexual markers to emphasize specific body parts; on the contrary, they serve to diffuse them. The only exception is one arbitrarily excised piece around the *derrière*, where the deeply red silk suddenly appears to fit as tightly as a glove, moulding and following every shape and movement – an arousing fragment. It highlights the potential sexiness of the dress, which through being merely suggested and then immediately withdrawn, comes across as all the more enticing and addictive.

Helmut Lang's fashion work shows skin at the expense of figure. It plays upon the theme of fabric as second skin. The received view of the sexiness of clothes rests upon an intentional exposure of skin as a clearly defined part of a clearly silhouetted figure. Clothes make people sexy by imparting significance to what is otherwise sensually meaningless, by transferring bare flesh into a code. The erotic moment, as Barthes has said, is unpredictable. Thus, eroticism would appear to be the result of a collapse of those codes by which the language of the body and the non-verbal communication of clothing can become predictable, known and comprehensible. It signals the flash of mere flesh or of that thing, to quote Hegel's phrase, which is 'merely sensually meaningless.' By contradistinction, as I have shown, the erotic moment does not come about through a sudden collapse of codes, but by a sophisticated transgression of them. The thrill of fashion is the thrill of that instant of surprise. The very codes that are transgressed can switch within an instant into new codifications, and the result is pure sexiness. It is this selfsame ephemeral quality of the fashion event that constitutes the essence of fashion. In the final analysis, rather than being a play upon the eternal stage of art, fashion's lot falls to dressing up mutton as lamb, or covering over and covering up the signs of decay that our fool flesh is heir to: Vanity within the sight of Death.

Notes

1. Georg Wilhelm Friedrich Hegel, *Ästhetik*, ed. Friedrich Bassenge, Frankfurt 1995, 2nd edition, vol. II, pp. 127/28.
2. Roland Barthes, *Le système de la mode*, Paris 1967, p. 261.
3. Hegel, *Ästhetik*, p. 128.
4. Anne Hollander, *Sex and Suits: The Evolution of Modern Dress*, New York 1994, p. 155.
5. Barthes, *Le système de la mode*, p. 261.

11

Martin Margiela: Signs of Time

Margiela, a member of the Antwerp school and the founder of deconstruction in fashion, is a master of reduction. In contrast to other designers, who make themselves into stars and set their face, their personality and their image to work as publicity for their fashion, Margiela does not allow himself to be photographed and makes no public appearances. He also does not sign his creations, sewing in a blank space at the place where the name would otherwise appear, a total paradox in a market completely captivated by the *griffe*. Two absences, two empty spaces, in a context in which image and name have become the dominant market strategies. Faceless, nameless.

Far from the inner-court of the Louvre, where twice a year the veil is lifted, and the secrets of the next season are displayed by the highest-paid models, Margiela's 'shows' take place in Barbès, for example, one of the poorest areas of Paris, inhabited mainly by Africans and Arabs, in empty Metro shafts, in deserted parking lots, in disused railway stations. His designs are often modeled by non-professionals who, instead of striding down the catwalk before an admiring public, mix with the audience, as in a modern theatrical staging, and only incidentally show the clothes in that they happen to be wearing them. Where the fashion industry establishment uses the image of the models to sell its clothes, Margiela models are considered, not as promotional devices, but as private people, and remain incognito. Anonymity is ostentatiously preserved by a strip printed over the eyes, or a thick veil, wrapped around the head. Instead of images, Margiela presents indexical signs – the signs of wear, among others.

Margiela applies his deconstructive talent to the subversion of the strategies of the present-day fashion scene. Perhaps more radically still than Kawakubo, his work aims at conquering a distance from the idea of fashion itself. His contribution to the exhibition, 'Le monde selon ses créateurs' is a carefully constructed allegory of this literally negative relation to fashion: presented in beaming white photographic negatives, Margiela's fashion appears as if under all-pervading x-rays that press under the surface, and let invisible elements come to light. In his work, two of the constitutive elements of fashion – perfect, invisible handicraft, and the product of this skill, the fulfilled, magical moment of the ephemeral appearance – are abandoned, unmasked, undermined. The traces of slow labor, of the production process and of the staging, all completely effaced in the blinding moment of the showing, are now exposed. In this exposure, there is more at work, however, than the disclosure of the secrets of the trade. Felix Salgado, who has spoken of 'decodification' and 'dissection' in Margiela's fashion, emphasizes the aggressive moment in Margiela's work through a scandalous comparison. It is as if Margiela lifts the skirt of Paris, and airs a terrible, frightening secret. If fashion is a process in which the feminine body is disguised as a fetish in order to conceal its alarming sexedness, then Margiela's is indeed a deconstructive work, bringing the secret of fashion to light, exposing the bland perfection of the disguise, deconstructing the product of fashion, the fetishized feminine body.

Margiela, a Belgian designer – to French ears, this is almost an oxymoron – found his own style with the discovery of a peculiarly Flemish trace at the heart of French elegance. The leitmotif of his work is the *mannequin*, in low Flemish, the *mannekin*: the cloth or wooden doll in the studio of the designer. The *mannekin* is the most important tool of the dressmaker, and its influence on the design process is so far-reaching that the women who model the clothes, and who are named after it, could be said merely to bring this 'little man' to life. It is not surprising, then, that Margiela's deconstruction of fashion begins with the native *mannekin*. The standardization of the female form, accomplished by the mannequin, represents the norms of classical proportion, as canonically transmitted through Greek sculpture. But, on the other hand, this also means that the classical statue has been shrunken to the tailor's measure, has become nothing but a *mannekin*. Margiela drags the *mannekin* out of the 'obscene' beyond of the fashion show, and into the lights of the stage, showing how the uniform, ideal body of the woman is produced by the art of the dressmaker, rather than being an incarnation of nature. The body is artificial, and the art of the dressmaker consists in making this artifice appear as natural, just as the model embodies the doll's body with her own living body.

Margiela shows that the origin of the unified whole body, in its classical form, lies in the cutting up of the material. He dresses women as the 'mannekins' that they embody: his finished clothes, in which hems and dart are external and visible, look like they are pinned up on a cloth doll. The irony is not the suggestion of the woman as doll, but the doll as 'woman,' as the woman that women are not. These 'unfinished' pieces expose the fascination with the inanimate, with the statue as doll, as the hidden nexus of fashion. In postfashion, this process is laid open and reversed, turned inside out. The lifeless model appears as a living person, and conversely, the living human body appears as *mannekin*, as cloth doll. The fetishistic core of fashion, its soul or, rather, its soullessness, is no longer disguised as the veil of truth or the garment of nature. In Margiela, this soul is presented as the 'ghost in the machine,' in the term of the philosopher Gilbert Ryle for the modern Cartesian myth of man, here the ghost that haunts the machinery of dressmaking, and that fashion successfully promotes and sells as 'woman.' In his fashion, we walk around ostentatiously just as we were 'fabricated.' Turning this core of fashion outwards, Margiela's clothes no longer animate the eternal perfection of a lifeless ideal. Rather we wear this ideal, conscious of it as something fabricated and lifeless, in order that we can live ourselves as something other than this, alongside it. In a second step, Margiela wraps us up in this 'other': no longer in the normativized, immortal ideal, but in the imprint that the organic living body had left behind. His 'rag clothes' show the traces that other bodies, in the course of their life, as the way to death, have left behind and impressed upon them.

From the technical point of view, this takes place in a number of discrete steps. First the inner dimension of the dress is turned outward. The jealously guarded secrets of production, the hem, the dart, etc. come to the surface; hidden functional accessories, such as zips or press studs are emphatically visible. Then the clothes are not worked through to a finished state; the ends of the fabric, for example, are not over-edged. The individual phases of the process of production remain visible in the smallest details. It is only to a first impression that this process recalls the functionalism of the Russian avant-garde of the 1920s, which allowed no other ornament than the functional itself. 'Aesthetic aspects must be replaced by the process of sewing itself,' declared Varvara Stepanova, a Russian designer, to the members of her studio: 'Let me explain. Do not put any ornamentation on the dress: the seams which are essential for the cut give the dress form: expose how the dress is put together, the zips and so on, just as such things are visible on a machine.'[1] For Margiela, it is less a matter of the aestheticization of a form. He deconstructs this functionalism, since in his work the function without a function also becomes an ornament: he is actually more on the side of *l'art pour l'art*. The turning outward of the production process is, for him, a turning-outwards of time. The elements of time that the dressmaker's art covers over, denies and sublimates into the present moment, are thematized in the exposure of the means. The impression of the unfinished is underlined by the fashion show. This new art of the unfinished is not to be confused with the *negligé* or the *beau désordre*, as it has been codified since the eighteenth century, in opposition to the *grande toilette*, to connote intimacy or eroticism. Margiela's women, by contrast, seem not 'dressed' in a strange way, in a way that corresponds to no recognizable codification.

Time clings to Margiela's work. His clothes carry the traces which time leaves behind, and are themselves signs of time. Time has entered into them in two respects: 1. as the time of the production process: and 2. as traces, which time leaves behind in the fabric in the course of use. This is not a reflection of the rise of recycling as a moral and a political imperative. Rather, these works have made the signs of time into their theme in a quite literal way. There are skirts made out of the kind of scarves that can be collected at a flea market; clothes made out of old clothes which have been taken apart and then put back together again; pullovers made out of old stockings, in which the heels model the breasts and the elbows; inner-linings made out of cotton which still bears the traces of the hoof-like shoes of the models, dipped in red dye, from the last show. Even if Margiela himself designates this procedure as recycling, it is not here a matter of an ethical operation, or of a political–ecological consciousness. To the contrary, it is clear that it is not a moral, but an entirely aesthetic maneuver. Margiela does not remake the old out of new materials, he uses the old and the used, as it was. In the process, he wins for his fashion something which is *per* definition foreign to fashion, something which was exclusively reserved to the artwork: the fascination of the single piece. Every piece that is made according to this method, regardless of how many versions there may be, is a unique piece, because the materials that are used in it are unique. No scarf is like the other, no foot-imprint is identical with another. Since the piece has taken time into itself, Margiela can hope that the traces of time will complete the work: it can age like a painting.

Here we see a distinctive approach to a problem that has to be encountered by all designers who work after and against the hundred-year fashion. For all innovative designers oppose themselves to the fashion of the seasons, with their rhythm, by which the fashion of tomorrow turns today's fashion into yesterday's fashion. Margiela has succeeded in the paradoxical assignment of initiating a fashion based on duration, rather than on change. Issey Miyake was the first to present a permanent collection, alongside the changing collections. Yamamoto dreams that clothes could become index-like signs for individuals. Kawakubo always emphasized that her clothes do not go out of fashion, but are made forever. As a counterweight to an economic form in the grip of dizzying consumption-frenzy, manifesting itself in a particularly merciless form in the bi- or tri-annual collections of fashion, many designers have sought to create a counter-rhythm. The rhythm of fashion having passed over into the whole realm of cultural production, to books, films, themes, images, architecture, fashion has now become the domain to show the greatest resistance to every form of merely fashion-driven change. Margiela has most effectively thematized this resistance. Like Miyake, he takes up in each collection emblematic designs and accessories from earlier collections; but he also introduces the age of the fabric and fragmentary citations as factors into his work, traces of time which hold up return as the mirror to change.

What makes Margiela's clothes truly unique, as unique as those of the *haute couture*, even as they stand the principles of the latter on its head, is the revaluation of the act of cutting to measure on the doll. The relationship of the body to the dress-maker's dummy is reversed. For the *haute couture*, the aim was to fit a reproducible design, created on the dummy, to an individual body, and to do this in a way such as to hide its weak points and to bring it as close as possible to the perfection of the classical statue. Margiela's art no longer cuts with ideal proportions in mind, in order to cover the flaws of individuals and to set in motion our inner classical statue. On the contrary, he traces the ideal measure of the mannekin onto the individual body, which thus can only appear as divergence from ideality. In deconstructing these mechanisms and the fascination with the inorganic which keeps them in movement, he creates, on the other side of the fetishized body of the doll, the space for the individual in the imprint of the body beyond the statue – without renouncing the fetishistic attraction. The question remains open as to how successful this other side is in comparison with his impressive dismantling of the old machinery of fashion.

From the conceptual point of view, Margiela's new individualism follows directly from the deconstructed *mannekin*. The uniqueness of his clothes lies in the indexical structure of the imprint of the individual body. In an entirely Benjamin-ean sense, Margiela's fashion becomes in this way what it wanted to be: authentic. The fashion designer as rag collector: thus the circle has closed and we are once again in Baudelaire's Paris, and the second half of the nineteenth century. With Benjamin, Margiela could say: 'Method of this project: literary montage. I needn't say anything. Merely show. I shall purloin no valuables, appropriate no ingenious formulations. But the rags, the refuse – these I will not inventory but allow, in the only way possible, to come into their own: by making use of them.'[2]

Nonetheless, at the high point of Margiela's career, there stands an antique statue of an altogether particular kind, figuring as a provisional and paradoxically transitory emblem of a radicalized aesthetic. With the 'new classic' we leave the realm of fashion and enter a realm of art – though an artistic realm which deconstructively crosses itself out, and which is devoted not to the eternal preservation of the museum, but rather deliberately calculates the self-destruction of the artwork. In the Boijmans Van Beuningen Museum in Rotterdam, Margiela's dressmaker's dummy was not only exposed to wind and rain but, under consultation with a microbiologist, was also subjected to yet harsher conditions through the application of a specific bacterial strain (Figure 14). This controlled decomposition changed over into a new, old aesthetic, an uncanny image of the classical statue,

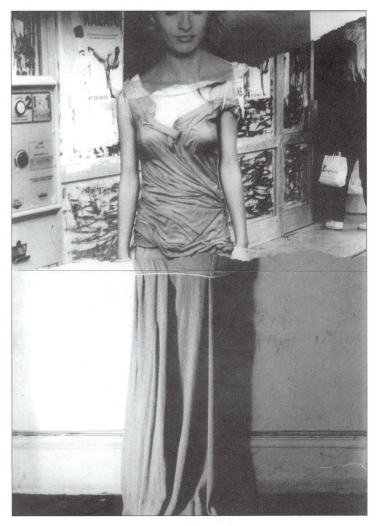

Figure 14
Martin Margiela, 1997, in
La maison Martin Margiela:
(9/4/1615), Museum
Boijmans Van Beuningen,
Rotterdam, © Maison
Martin Margiela.

the epitome of the eternal, here not in radiant white marble, but produced through fungus attack:

> a doll wears a very wide dress, over which is drawn a transparent, hip-length net T-shirt made of nylon; apparently intentionally, the tight T-shirt lays the dress in graceful, lightly diagonal running folds, without pressing them flat. The whole dress is covered with a greenish mold. The effect is of a Greek statue, something that looks as classical as if Phidias himself had worked on it.[3]

The jacket in Figure 15 is made from an almost old-fashioned traditional 'Pepper and Salt' woven wool-cloth, as is classically used for men's suits. It closes off tightly around the waist, and sits

Figure 15
Martin Margiela, 1995,
© Steel Stillman.

closely on the upper body, as if poured on. A continuous black zip is sewed on, not hidden. That which is normally concealed between the lining and the fabric is turned outward. The hem and the dart stand on the outside, and show that they could not have been more perfectly finished. The breasts are clearly profiled, in a star-shaped pattern. The impression of the dummy, on which the material is pinned up according to the proportions of the customer, is reinforced by the untreated cotton lining, a material ordinarily used to try out a particular cut or to prepare the pattern for a dress. This inconspicuous lining is also finished, as if it were a matter of the outer side of the dress: the edges are generously pressed and the seams are covered, the zip sewed in from inside. The neck and shoulder parts are strengthened in the manner of old-fashioned men's suits, with a very fine black, ribbed, satin-like viscose material.

The arms of the jacket demonstrate the exact opposite of the careful fit: they are of an undefined excess length, and also double the necessary width. On a dummy, they would dangle down hopelessly like the arms of a marionette, underlining the point of the piece. The buttons follow the model of the old-fashioned classical suit, but are double the normal size. Although they are purely decorative, they can be opened. Their old-fashioned good-quality makes for a strange contrast with the very prosaic zips. Tending slightly towards the pompous, the sleeves are perfectly and discreetly tailored. Their lustrous white viscose lining slides on the arms, so that the material lays in heavy folds. In the all but majestic fall of the folds, these sleeves cite from afar the props of the official masculine dignity of a past era: they recall the robes of the high court, the gown of the university, the vestments of the church. It is hard to accept the connection of these sleeves with the outwards-turned mannequin-top, and indeed, one can promptly take them off. The sleeves are fastened with large press studs, attached, as if hastily and by hand, with white tacking thread. These studs, which stylistically mediate between the torso and the arm, can be undone in two different ways: one can just let them hang down behind, so that the arms have their freedom of movement; or one can have them lie completely to the side. In the latter case, all that is left is the vest-like close-fitting top, and the effect is decidedly unfinished; very short hanging sleeves, reinforced by a small round shoulder padding ring, remain behind: they are in the end not over-edged.

The jacket does not bear the name of the designer. In the place of the signature there is once again a blank white cotton label affixed with tacking thread, of the kind that children used to have attached to their clothes, with their name written upon it, so it would not get mixed up with someone else's.

This creation has a double frame of reference: in the first place, it stands before the background of fashion design, in the second place before that of the traditional classical strict men's suit. The connotation of professionality implied by this latter reference is reinforced by the citation of a still more formal mode of signifying masculine professional authority, that of the judge's or professor's robe. Such relatively uniform modes of dress, with their discreet elegance and their proper finish, have the function, among others, of distracting attention from the specificity of the individual's body, of neutralizing its presence. The tailor's art here consists in bringing body and clothing to disappear before the man conscious of his responsibility. Now, however, this body becomes insistently visible, disguised as a pure body, mindless and lifeless, as a dummy.

On this background, it is the jacket which, in an initial moment, first brings the body into play. Attention is heightened by the disruption of the horizon of expectations. The body – the torso and arms – are in clothed in diametrically opposite ways: the one tight, the other wide; fullness of material is contrasted with utmost minimality, old-fashioned quality and perfection in the finish with the unfinished, merely sketched out pattern. The impression this produces is by no means harmonious: the body is not brought out as a whole, as an organic unit; rather, its divisibility, the possibility of isolating particular limbs, as utilized, for example, in jazz dance, is underlined.

In a second step, the masculine and the feminine body, and also the question of feminine authority, are brought into a new context. In the close-fitting top, in which the breasts are emphasized through the stitching, there lies clearly a physical body, whose erotic connotations are marked by the continuous zip. The sheer materiality of the physicality is emphasized, but at the same time ironized, by the fact that the outfit seems to be pinned onto a doll. Through the stitching it becomes clear that it is not a matter of a natural but of an artificial body. The classic feminine fashion, always concerned with an effective underlining of 'feminine charm,' achieved, often enough, by allowing a generous glance into the *decolleté* – the whole play, in short, along precisely defined borders of hiding, exhibiting, letting oneself be seen – is thematized and humorously commented on by the sudden and unexpected sight of an erotically uncharged zone: with certain movements, the jacket allows a glance from behind at the upper arm. The mechanism is summoned up, but it is devoid of content. In this way, it becomes clear that it is the mechanism itself, and not the question of whether or not there is anything to see, which is erotically charged.

The wearer of this jacket, then, is not dressed like a man, nor is it simply a matter of men's fashion being eroticized and feminized. Rather, the impression that there is no body underneath these garments is retrospectively denounced as a fiction: the male suit is de-sublimated, in that it is designed as women's clothing is designed, in order to reveal rather than to conceal the body. Moreover, the feminine body is exhibited as a fabricated rather than a natural body, and the mechanism of hiding and revealing by which this body is eroticized is reflected upon and ironized by the exposure of the way that it continues to operate even without any content to hide and reveal. The mythology of sexually neutral identity is shattered by the ironic staging of the feminine body. The woman can smilingly assume the inheritance of the venerable insignia of male authority, unquestionably dressed in 'professional clothing,' precisely through the fact that she undoes this myth. For all this authority comes down in the end to nothing more than a *mannekin*.

The other background before which the jacket stands, we have said, is that of fashion itself; clearly the design is highly self-reflexive. At the center of fashion lies the art of producing an effect without revealing the manner in which it is produced. Like a magician, fashion conceals its tricks. Its seduction lies not least in the surprise of this unbelievable success; it includes a moment of curiosity on the side of the spectator. The theatricality of fashion lies in its ability to create a perfect staged moment.

By contrast, postfashion, for which the jacket of Margiela stands as an exemplary instance, is not an art of the moment. Rather, it takes as its object the temporality and the historicity of fashion as a process. On the one hand, it exposes the various steps of the process by which an article of clothing is produced, and records them. It captures the truly ephemeral (as opposed to the artificial ephemerality of fashion), that which was always supposed to disappear without trace: the sheer materiality of the cloth in the unfinished support-sleeves; the dressmaker's dummy; the condition of the top as seen within, pinned up in a way such that one could now begin to sew it together; the haste and provisionality expressed by the press studs attached with the white tacking thread; the sleeve arm that, after an artful cutting out, lovingly worked out in every detail, is quickly sewn up – a perfection in the functional detail, which comes out so much the more starkly in that it is here functionless, *l'art pour l'art*. The ornament here lies in the luxurious superficiality of the function. To the perfect moment of illusion, the jacket opposes the arduous work that goes to produce the illusion.

On the other hand, the historical development of the genre 'dressmaking,' through which particular effects first became possible, also comes into the foreground. In an almost encyclopedic gesture, the work features three different modes of 'closure,' corresponding to three stages in the historical development of dressmaking: button, press stud, zip, whereby one of the decisive advantages of the last two, namely their relative invisibility, is called up *ex negativo* by their being drastically put on display. Against the extra-temporal effect of the sudden success of fashion, stands here the historical development of technical details which had made such triumphs possible in the first place.

Margiela's fashion lifts the skirt of the city of Paris. It raises the veil on a past, false ideality. From under this veil the secret of fashion steps forth: the fetishistic structure of desire. The fetish, which, according to Benjamin, underlies the sex appeal of the inorganic, is the heart of fashion. This is why fashion was the site at which the lifeless was animated, without having to bear the stigmata of life, at which the idea came to life, hard, flawless, complete and perfect like the marble of the antique statues, alive for the perfect moment of the illusion. Postfashion brings this fetishistic core to light: it exposes it. Margiela does this in a particularly drastic way; he shows how fashion brought the ideal to life, an ideal which, however, was as such located out of time, untouched, like the dummy, by the decline to which the flesh is subject. Time will not stand still, however, and the disfiguration of the ideal has inevitably to be followed by a refiguration. The rag-collecting aspect of the fashion of Margiela points to the reconstructive attempt to rethink clothes as the signs of an individual, unique life and death.

Notes

1. Varvara Stepanova, 'The dress of today is the industrial dress' (1923), cited by Isabelle Anscombe, *A Woman's Touch: Women in Design from 1860 to the Present Day*, New York 1984, p. 96.
2. Walter Benjamin, *The Arcades Project*, Cambridge 1999, (Convolut 'On the Theory of Knowledge, Theory of Progress'), N1a, 8, p. 460.
3. Anja Seeliger, under the fine title, 'Die Pilze des Schönen,' *taz*, 4 July 1997, p. 16, in which of course the Baudelairean *Flowers of Evil* are present.

Select Bibliography

Alewyn, Richard and Karl Sälzle (1959), *Das große Welttheater – Die Epoche der höfischen Feste in Dokument und Deutung*, Hamburg.

Anscombe, Isabelle (1984), *A Woman's Touch: Women in Design from 1860 to the Present Day*, New York.

Apter, Emily (1991), *Feminizing the Fetish – Psychoanalysis and Narrative Obsession in Turn-of-the-Century France*, Ithaca.

ART/Fashion (Firenze, Biennale 1996), New York Guggenheim Museum, Soho.

Barthes, Roland (1967), *Le système de la mode*, Paris; (1990), *The Fashion System*, trans. Matthew Ward and Richard Howard, Berkeley.

Baudelaire, Charles (1975), *Œuvres complètes*, vol. 1, ed. Claude Pichois, Paris.

Beauvoir, Simone de (1949), *Le deuxième sexe*, vol. 2, Paris.

Benjamin, Walter (1969), 'On some motifs in Baudelaire,' in *Illuminations*, ed. and with an introduction by Hannah Arendt, trans. Harry Zohn, New York.

—— (1999), *The Arcades Project*, trans. Howard Eiland and Kevin McLaughlin, Cambridge.

Bieber, Margarete (1977), *Ancient Copies: Contributions to the History of Greek and Roman Art*, New York.

Blau, Herbert (1999), *Nothing in itself – Complexions of Fashion*, Bloomington.

Bocca, Nicoletta (ed.) (1990), *Moda: Poesia e progetto*, Milan.

Boehn, Max von (1923), *Die Mode*, Munich.

Boucher, François (1965), *2000 ans de mode*, Paris.

Bourdieu, Pierre (1989), *Distinction: A Social Critique of the Judgment of Taste*, trans. Richard Nice, Cambridge, MA.

—— and Yvette Delsaut (1975), 'Le couturier et sa griffe,' in *Actes de la recherche en sciences sociales* 1.

Bovenschen, Sylvia (ed.) (1985), *Die Listen der Mode*, Frankfurt.

Brassens, Georges, *Georges Brassens par excellence IV* (Philips C-72-CX-253).

Butler, Judith (1990), *Gender Trouble. Feminism and the Subversion of Identity*, New York.

Delbourg-Delphis, Marylène (1981), *Le Chic et le Look*, Paris.

Deslandres, Yvonne (1976), *Le costume, image de l'homme*, Paris.

Du Rosselle, Bruno (1980), *La Mode*, Paris.

Evans, Carolyn (1999) '"Masks, Mirrors and Mannequins": Elsa Schiaparelli and the De-centered Subject,' in *Fashion Theory* 3, 1.

—— (2001) 'The Enchanted Spectacle,' in *Fashion Theory* 5, 3.

Faulkner, William (1923, 1955), *Mosquitoes*, New York.

Felman, Shoshana (1981), 'Rereading Femininity,' in *Yale French Studies* 62.

Flugel, J.C. (1930), *The Psychology of Clothes*, London.

Fouqué, Caroline de la Motte (1987), *Geschichte der Moden 1785–1829. Ein Beitrag zur Geschichte der Zeit*, Berlin.

Garber, Magerie (1992), *Vested Interests – Cross Dressing & Cultural Anxiety*, New York.

Garelick, Rhonda (1998), *Rising Star: Dandyism, Genre, and Performance in the Fin de Siècle*, Princeton.

Garve, Christian (1978), *Über die Moden*, Frankfurt.

Gaultier, Jean-Paul (1990), *A nous deux, la mode*, Paris.

Godfrey, Sima (1989), 'Haute Couture and Haute Culture,' in *A New History of French Literature*, ed. Denis Hollier, Cambridge, MA.

Gottwald, Laura and Janusz (1970), *Frederick's of Hollywood 1947–73 – 26 Years of Mail Order Seduction*, New York.

Harms, Ingeborg (ed.) (2000), *Figurationen. Gender, Literatur, Kultur*, 2: Mode/Kunst, Cologne.

—— (2000), 'Hardbody – Softbody. Die Schönheit trägt Waffen,' in *Figurationen* 2: Mode/Kunst.

Haverkamp, Anselm (2002), 'Dialektisches Bild,' in *Figura cryptica. Theorie der literarischen Latenz*, Frankfurt, pp. 56–70.

Hayward Gallery (1998), *Addressing the Century – 100 Years of Art & Fashion*, London.

Heine, Heinrich (1998), *Journey to Italy*, ed. Christopher Johnson, trans. Charles G. Leland, New York.

Hollander, Anne (1975), *Seeing Through Clothes*, New York.

—— (1995), *Sex and Suits: The Evolution of Modern Dress*, New York.

James, Henry, (1867, 1981), *The American*, New York.

Koda, Harold (1985), 'Rei Kawakubo and the Aesthetic of Poverty,' in *Dress*, New York.

—— and Richard Martin (1989), *The Historical Mode – Fashion and Art in the 1980s*, New York.

——, Richard Martin and Laura Sinderbrand (eds) (1987), *Three Women: Madeleine Vionnet, Claire McCardell, and Rei Kawakubo*, New York.

König, René (1971), *Macht und Reiz der Mode*, Vienna, Düsseldorf.

Kozasu, Atsuko (ed.) (1988–91), *Six*, No. 1–9, Tokyo.

Lacan, Jacques (1966), *Ecrits*, Paris.

Landfester, Ulrike (1995), *Der Dichtung Schleier – Zur poetischen Funktion von Kleidung in Goethes Frühwerk*, Freiburg.

Laurent, Yves Saint (1988), *Images of Design 1958–1988*, with an introduction by Marguerite Duras, New York.

Lehmann, Ulrich (2001), *Tigersprung. Fashion in Modernity*, Cambridge.

Lehnert, Gertrud (ed.) (1998), *Mode, Weiblichkeit und Modernität*, Dortmund.

—— (1998), *Frauen machen Mode*, Dortmund.

Lemoine-Luccioni, Eugenie (1983), *La Robe: Essai psychanalytique sur le vêtement*, Paris.

Leopardi, Giacomo (1824, 1999), *Operette Morali*, Milan.

Leymaire, Jean (1987), *Chanel*, Geneva.

Link-Heer, Ursula (1998), 'Die Mode im Museum oder Manier und Stil (mit einem Blick auf Versace),' in *Mode, Weiblickeit und Modernität*, ed. Gertrud Lehnert, Dortmund.

Lipovetsky, Gilles (1987), *L'empire de l'éphémère: La mode et son destin dans les sociétés modernes*, Paris.

Loos, Adolf (1982), *Spoken into the Void: Collected Essays 1897–1900*, trans. Jane Newman and John Smith, Cambridge.

Loschek, Ingrid (1998), *Mode Designer – Ein Lexikon von Armani bis Yamamoto*, Munich.

Marcadé, Bernarc and Dan Cameron (eds) (1997), *Pierre & Gilles – The Complete Works*, Cologne.

Margiela, Martin (1997), *La maison Martin Margiela: (9/4/1615)*, ed. Museum Boijmans Van Beuningen, exhibition catalogue, Museum Boijmans Van Beuningen, Rotterdam.

Marley, Diane de (1980), *The History of Haute Couture 1850–1950*, New York.

Martin, Richard (ed.) (1997), *The St. James Encyclopedia of Fashion – A Survey of Style from 1945 to the Present*, Detroit.

Marx, Karl (1927), *Der achtzehnte Brumaire des Louis Bonaparte*, with an introduction by Friedrich Engels, ed. D. Rjazanov, Vienna, Berlin.

Meinecke, Thomas (1998), *Tomboy*, Frankfurt.

Mentges, Gabriele (1995), 'Der Mensch nach Maß – der vermessene Mensch,' in *Moden und Menschen*, Stuttgart.

Miyake, Issey (1978), *East meets West*, Tokyo.

Montesquieu, Charles Secondat Baron de (1952), *The Spirit of Laws*, in *Encyclopedia Britannica*, ed. William Benton, Chicago.

Morand, Paul (1976), *L'allure de Chanel*, Paris.

Musée de la Mode et du Costume (1984), *De la mode et des lettres du XIIIe siècle à nos jours*, Paris.

—— (1991), *Le monde selon ses créateurs*, Paris.

Musil, Robert (1929, 1978), *Die Frau gestern und morgen*, in *Gesammelte Werke*, vol. 8, Hamburg.

Parinaud, André (1981), *The Unspeakable Confession of Salvador Dali*, New York.

Pastoureau, Michel (1991), *L'étoffe du Diable – Une histoire des rayures et des tissus rayés*, Paris.

Perrot, Philippe (1981), *Les dessus et les dessous de la bourgeoisie*, Paris.

—— (1984), *Le corps féminin: XVIII et XIX siècles, Le travail des apparences*, Paris.

Poiret, Paul (1930, 1974), *En habillant l'époque*, Paris.

Poschardt, Ulf (1998), *Anpassen*, Hamburg.

Richard, Birgit (1995), *Todesbilder – Kunst, Subkultur, Medien*, Munich.

Rousseau, Jean-Jacques (1964), *La Nouvelle Héloïse*, in *Œuvres complètes*, eds Bernard Gagnebin and Marcel Raymond, Paris.

—— (1979) *Emile or On Education*, ed. Allan Bloom, New York.

—— (1987) *Politics and the Arts – Letter to M. D'Alembert on the Theatre*, trans. with notes and an introduction by Allan Bloom, Ithaca.

Sander, August (1980), *Menschen des 20. Jahrhunderts – Portraitphotographien 1892–1952*, ed. Gunther Sander, Munich.

Schiaparelli, Elsa (1954), *Shocking Life*, London.

Schickedanz, Hans J. (1980), *Der Dandy*, Dortmund.

Schlaffer, Hannelore (1991), 'Emanzipierte Mode und deutscher Pietismus,' in *Freibeuter* 48, pp. 56-60.

Seeliger, Anja (1997), 'Die Pilze des Schönen,' in *taz*, 4 July.

Simmel, Georg (1919), 'Die Mode,' in *Philosophische Kultur*, Leipzig.

Simon, Philippe (1936), *Monographie d'une industrie de luxe: La haute couture*, Paris.

Sombart, Werner (1922, 1983), *Liebe, Luxus und Kapitalismus – Über die Entstehung der modernen Welt aus dem Geist der Verschwendung*, Berlin.

Sommer, Ingrid (ed.) (1974), *Der Fortgang der Tugend und des Lasters: Daniel Chodowieckis Monatskupfer zum Göttinger Taschenkalender mit Erklärungen Georg Christoph Lichtenbergs 1778–1783*, Berlin.

Steele, Valerie (1991), *Women of Fashion: Twentieth-Century Designers*, New York.

—— (1996), *Fetish – Fashion, Sex and Power*, New York.

—— (2001), *The Corset: A Cultural History*, New Haven.

Sudjic, Deyan (1990), *Rei Kawakubo and Comme des Garçons*, New York.

Taylor, Marc C. (1997), *Hiding*, Chicago.

Texte zur Kunst (1997), 25: Mode.

Thiel, Erika (1980), *Geschichte des Kostüms*, East Berlin.

Veblen, Thorstein (1919), *The Theory of the Leisure Class – An Economic Study of Institutions*, New York.

Vinken, Barbara (ed.) (1992), *Dekonstruktiver Feminismus – Literaturwissenschaft in Amerika*, Frankfurt.

Vischer, Friedrich Theodor (1879), *Mode und Cynismus – Beiträge zur Kenntnis unserer Culturformen und Sittenbegriffe*, Stuttgart.

Weidmann, Heiner (1998), 'Kleidermoden, Moden der Gestik. Ein Versuch zur praktischen Erinnerung,' in *Colloquium Helveticum* 27: Memoria.

—— (2000), 'Kleider lesen,' in *Passagen/ Passages* 29, 4–7.

Wilson, Elizabeth (1985), *Adorned in Dreams: Fashion and Modernity*, Berkeley.

Wolter, Gundula (1995), 'Lieber sterb' ich, als meiner Frau die Hose zu lassen: Zur Kulturgeschichte der Frauenhose', in *Moden und Menschen*, Stuttgart.

Worth, Gaston (1895), *La Couture et la confection des vêtements de femme*, Paris.

Yonnet, Paul (1986), *Jeux, modes et masses*, Paris.

Zeffirelli, Franco (1986), *Zeffirelli – An Autobiography*, New York.

Index